Code Copying

Brill's Studies in Language, Cognition and Culture

Series Editors

Alexandra Y. Aikhenvald (*Centre for Indigenous Health Equity Research, Central Queensland University*)
R.M.W. Dixon (*Centre for Indigenous Health Equity Research, Central Queensland University*)
N.J. Enfield (*University of Sydney*)

VOLUME 38

The titles published in this series are listed at *brill.com/bslc*

Code Copying

The Strength of Languages in Take-over and Carry-over Roles

By

Lars Johanson

BRILL

LEIDEN | BOSTON

Cover illustration: Design by Celine van Hoek

The Library of Congress Cataloging-in-Publication Data is available online at https://catalog.loc.gov
LC record available at https://lccn.loc.gov/2023024198

Typeface for the Latin, Greek, and Cyrillic scripts: "Brill". See and download: brill.com/brill-typeface.

ISSN 1879-5412
ISBN 978-90-04-54843-5 (hardback)
ISBN 978-90-04-54845-9 (e-book)

Copyright 2023 by Lars Johanson. Published by Koninklijke Brill NV, Leiden, The Netherlands.
Koninklijke Brill NV incorporates the imprints Brill, Brill Nijhoff, Brill Hotei, Brill Schöningh, Brill Fink, Brill mentis, Vandenhoeck & Ruprecht, Böhlau, V&R unipress and Wageningen Academic.
Koninklijke Brill NV reserves the right to protect this publication against unauthorized use. Requests for re-use and/or translations must be addressed to Koninklijke Brill NV via brill.com or copyright.com.

This book is printed on acid-free paper and produced in a sustainable manner.

Contents

    Preface   IX
    Acknowledgements   XI
    List of Figures and Examples   XII
    Abbreviations   XIV
    Notations   XV
    Transcription   XVI

1   The Code-Copying Model   1
    1   Introduction   1
    2   Basic Code and Model Code   1
    3   Take-over and Carry-over Copying   2
    4   Code Switching and Code Mixing   2
    5   Global and Selective Copying   3
    6   The Contact Globe   5
    7   The Order of Influence   5
    8   Copying Is a Creative Act   6
    9   Attractiveness   7
    10   Contact Processes   8
    11   Extremely High Levels of Copying   8
    12   Historical Stratification   9
    13   Distinguishing Carry-over and Take-over Copying   11
    14   Example of Carry-over Copying: Linguistic Convergence in the Volga Area   13

2   Global Copies   18

3   Selective Copies   21
    1   Selective Copying of Material/Phonological Features   21
    2   Selective Copying of Semantic Features   22
    3   Selective Copying of Combinational Features   22
    4   Semantic-Combinational Copies   25
        4.1   *Postpositions Modelled on Prepositional Patterns*   25
        4.2   *Combinational Copying in Clause Junction*   26
    5   Selective Copying of Frequential Patterns   29
        5.1   *Frequential Copies in Clause Junction*   31
    6   Mixed Copies   32
        6.1   *Mixed Copies with Junctors*   33

		7	Distributional Classes 34
		8	Degree of Complexity 35
		9	Accommodation of Copies 35

4 **Code-Copying and Grammaticalization** 37
    1 Isomorphism 37
    2 Combined Scheme 38
    3 Aikhenvald's 'Grammatical Accommodation' as a Case of Selective Copying 39
    4 Diachronic Processes Are Not Copiable 42
    5 Lexical and Grammatical Targets of Copying 43
    6 Awareness of Sources 44
    7 Use after Copying 45
    8 'Inherited Grammaticalization' 46
    9 Conceivable Carry-over-Copying of Evidentials 47

5 **Remodeling Languages** 49
    1 Code-Internal Development 49
    2 Remodeling the Basic-Code Frame 49
    3 Convergence and Divergence 50
    4 Converging through Selective Copying 51
    5 Momentary, Habitualized, and Conventionalized Copies 52

6 **Turkic Family-External Contacts** 54

7 **Code-Copying in Some Large Languages of the World** 60
    1 English 60
    2 Chinese 61
    3 Arabic 62
    4 Russian 64

8 **Stability** 66

9 **High-Copying Codes** 68
    1 Examples of High-Copying Languages 68
    2 Attitudes towards High-Copying Varieties 70

10 **Cognates and Copies** 72
    1 Distinctions between Cognates and Copies 73
    2 Motivations for Copying Bound Morphemes 74

    3   Cognates and Copies in Altaic Verb Derivation   74
    4   Copies   75
    5   Evidence   76
    6   Arguments from Silence   77
    7   Copies and Copiability   78
    8   Superstable Morphology?   78
    9   Typological Arguments   79

11   Types of Copying in Written Languages   80
    1   Types 1 and 2: Take-over and Carry-over Copying   82
    2   Subtypes of Type 1 Take-over Copying   83
    3   Type 2: Carry-over Copying   84
    4   Type 3: Alternate Use of the Codes   85
    5   A Lower-Ranking Code Explicates Texts in Higher-Ranking Code   86
    6   Type 5: Higher Ranking Code as Graphic Representation of the Lower Ranking Code   87
    7   Examples of Type 1 Take-over Copying   88
        7.1   *Akkadian Take-over Influence on West Semitic*   88
        7.2   *Arabic Take-over Influence on New Persian*   89
        7.3   *New Persian Take-over Influence on High Ottoman*   91
        7.4   *New Persian Take-over Influence on Chaghatay*   96
    8   Examples of Type 2: Carry-over Copying   98
        8.1   *Prākrit Carry-over Influence on Deviant Sanskrit*   98
        8.2   *Indic Carry-over Influence on Deviant Written Chinese*   99
        8.3   *Japanese Carry-over Influence on Deviant Written Chinese*   100
        8.4   *Mongolian Carry-over Influence on Deviant Written Chinese*   102
        8.5   *Manchu Carry-over Influence on Deviant Written Chinese*   103
    9   Examples of Type 3: Alternate Use of the Codes   105
        9.1   *Mixed Poems*   105
        9.2   *Bilingual Hebrew-Romance Texts*   109
        9.3   *Manchu-Chinese Mixed Poetry*   109
        9.4   *Mixed Text Types in Medieval British Writing*   109
    10   Examples of Type 4: Lower-Ranking Code Explicates Higher-Ranking Code   111
        10.1   *Japanese Reading Aids for Chinese Texts*   111
        10.2   *Burmese Reading Aids for Pali Texts*   112

- 10.3 *Sinhalese Reading Aids for Pali Texts* 114
- 10.4 *Karaim Reading Aids for Hebrew Texts* 114
11 Examples of Type 5: Higher-Ranking Code Represents Lower-Ranking Code 116
- 11.1 *Semitic Represented in Sumerian Writing* 117
- 11.2 *Other Codes Represented in Cuneiform Writing* 119
- 11.3 *Old Persian Represented in Elamite Writing* 120
- 11.4 *Middle Iranian Represented in Aramaic Writing* 121
- 11.5 *Japanese Represented in Chinese Writing* 123
12 A Passive-Active Scale 124

References 127
Index of Subjects 144
Index of Languages and Language Families 146
Index of Personal Names 148

Preface

The essay "Code Copying. The Strength of Languages in Take-over and Carry-over Roles" presents a new synthesis of my Code-Copying Model, an integrated framework for investigating contact-induced processes. The volume summarizes the model's principles and foundations in a clear, cogent, and coherent manner. The fundamental difference between 'take-over' copying and 'carry-over' copying is given special value. Speakers can take over copies from a secondary code into their own primary code or, alternatively, they can carry over copies from their own primary code into their variety of a secondary code. The results of these two types of copying are significantly different and thus provide insights into historical processes.

My own work on this topic started 30 years ago, and the model has thus been tested theoretically and empirically through many years studying the relevant issues. My purpose is to define a framework which includes all the main issues in their interrelationship. The terminology is kept intuitive and simple to apply. The model is demonstrated to be applicable to both spoken and written codes. Moreover, the model can be pertinent to describing non-linguistic copying processes, for instance, in cultural contexts.

This is a first innovative summary presenting all essential details of the Code-Copying Model. Over the years, numerous linguistic studies have applied the framework for analyzing contact-induced changes in different languages. This volume is a further logical step in the process of understanding the phenomena involved. It does not replace earlier contributions by other linguists.

The volume is not an introductory text, but rather provided for students of linguistics who already have a certain knowledge of the subject. The statements are illustrated from a wide range of languages. The prevalence of Turkic languages is due to the author's special interest in this language family, but illustrative examples from a large number of other languages demonstrate the validity of the model for the description of contact-induced phenomena in any language.

The aim is not to engage in debate. Code Copying has distinct bearing on human communication, cognition, categorization, and social conventions. It stands apart from the treatment of contact processes in other contributions, but it shows interrelations with them. The major focus is on the dynamics of contact-induced processes synchronically and through language history.

It has long been my desire to present the Code-Copying Model in a single monograph, but so far, my relevant research has only been available in studies published in journals and collections of essays. The series Research Perspectives: Linguistics provides an appropriate forum for realizing the plan to elaborate my views on the different aspects of the topic. The volume begins with a summary of the model's components, illustrates the types of copying with illustrative examples from Turkic and various other languages in the world. Bi-and multilingual large, English, Chinese, Arabic, Russian, and small high-copying languages provide examples of language contact scenarios. Individual chapters deal with questions of copiability of grammaticalization, stability of high-copying languages, and the difficulties in distinguishing between cognates and copies. My aim has been to demonstrate that copying is not 'dangerous', and does not lead to the death of languages. On the contrary, it is a creative, rule-governed process, which can increase the strength of the copying code by facilitating bi- or multilingual speakers' communication. The final chapter presents the phenomenon of language intertwining in written high-copying languages analyzed in the Code-Copying Model.

Lars Johanson

Acknowledgements

The publishing house John Benjamins has given permission to use the articles Lars Johanson "Remodelling grammar: Copying, conventionalization, grammaticalization" published in Siemund, Peter & Kintana, Noemi eds. 2008. *Language Contact and Contact Languages*, pp. 61–79. ISBN 978 90 272 1927 5, and Lars Johanson "Isomorphic processes: Grammaticalization and copying of grammatical elements" published in Robbeets, Martine & Cuyckens, Hubert eds. 2013. *Shared Grammaticalization. With Special Focus on the Transeurasian Languages*, pp. 101–109. ISBN 978 90 272 0599 5.

The publisher De Gruyter Mouton has given permission to use the article Johanson, Lars 2013. "Written language intertwining". In Bakker, Peter & Matras, Yaron eds. *Contact languages. A comprehensive guide*, pp. 273–331. Berlin & Boston: De Gruyter Mouton. ISBN 978-1-61451-476-3.

Figures and Examples

Figures

1. The contact globe   6
2. Selective grammatical copying   38
3. Copying dual markers   42

Examples

1. Global copy in Germany Turkish   3
2. Selective material copy in Norway Hungarian   4
3. Selective combinational copy in Northwest Karaim   4
4. Selective copy of a semantic feature   4
5. Regular Tatar and Common Turkic correspondences (Berta 1989)   16
6. Chuvash and Common Turkic correspondences   17
7. Kashkay copy of an Iranian enclitic marker   18
8. Irano-Turkic copies of Persian simple preposition + nominal core + iza:fat marker   19
9. Khalaj   19
10. Copied clausal adjunctors   20
11. Copying of case assignment in Germany Turkish   23
12. Copying constituent order   23
13. Khalaj   24
14. Standard Turkish   24
15. Kashkay   25
16. Southern Azeri   25
17. Turkish   27
18. Gagauz   28
19. Azeri   28
20. Tebriz Azeri   30
21. Tebriz Azeri   30
22. Tebriz Azeri   31
23. Tebriz Azeri   31
24. Mixed copies   32
25. Khalaj   32
26. Mixed copies   33
27. Germany Turkish   34

28	Germany Turkish	34
29	Copying the function of case marking in Northwest Karaim	43
30	Carried over syntactic features in Govorka	64
31	Carried over postpositional function in Govorka	64
32	Northwest Karaim	71
33	Ottoman prose	93
34	High-copying Ottoman sentence	93
35	Standard Turkish	94
36	High-copying Chaghatay	97
37	Medieval bilingual text	110
38	Hebrew Bible text	115
39	Japanese	124

Abbreviations

ABL	ablative		LOC	locative
ACC	accusative		N	noun
ADJ	adjective marker		NEG	negation
ADV	adverbial		OPT	optative
AOR	aorist		PASS	passive
CONJ	conjunction		PAST	past
CONV	converb		PL	plural
COP	copular particle		POSS	possessive
DAT	dative		POSTP	postposition
DEF	definite		PROP	propriative
DUAL	dual		PTCL	particle
FEM	feminine		REL	relator *ki*
GEN	genitive		Q	question particle
HYP	hypothetical		SG	singular
INF	infinitive		TOP	topic
INTRA	intraterminal		VN	verbal nominal
JUNCT	junctor		VOL	voluntative

In Hebrew

ABS	absolute state
BOTH	common gender
CONST	construct state
DEF	definite article
MASC	masculine
PIEL	verb form *piel*
PREP	preposition
PTCP	participle

Notations

Mathematical angle brackets ⟨ ⟩ are used for glosses in text, e.g. Turkish *at-lar* ⟨horse-PL⟩ 'horses'.

Curly brackets of the type {...} are used for morphophonemic formulas that summarize the possible realizations of bound morphemes, e.g. Turkish {-CI}. Optional elements are in brackets, e.g. Turkish {-(y)Im}. Capital letters in the formula mark morphophonemic variation.

Hyphens are often used to show the segmentation of complex forms, indicating the boundaries between constituent segments, usually, but not always, morphemes, e.g. Chuvash *Vul-ă-p* 'I will read'.

Simple arrows are used for morphological derivation. Thus ← means 'derived from', whereas → means 'derived as'.

Double arrows are used for copied (borrowed) elements. Thus ⇐ means 'copied from', whereas ⇒ means 'copied as'.

The sign < means 'developed from', whereas > means 'developed into'.

In translations, X is used as a shorthand for the 3SG personal pronouns 'he', 'she', 'it', 'him', 'her', e.g. Persian *Raft-e ast* 'X has gone'.

Transcription

Turkic examples are given in Turcological transcription as in Johanson (2021).
Quoted examples are mostly given in the same transcription as in the source.
Graphic forms representing official orthographies are given in angle brackets (chevrons), e.g. Turkish ‹çicek› 'flower'.
A dot under a vowel marks a lax vowel. Long vowels are marked by a triangular colon, e.g. *vaːr* 'existent' in Turkic, but with language specific notation in other languages, e.g. Persian *javān-ī*. Palatalized consonants are marked with ', e.g. Karaim *m'en'* 'I'.

CHAPTER 1

The Code-Copying Model

1   Introduction

This volume on Code Copying deals with linguistic contact-induced phenomena. It is the result of long-standing work on contact questions in an integrated model. The phenomena cover various kinds of influence, traditionally referred to as 'borrowing', 'calquing', 'replication', 'transfer', 'interference', 'importation', 'substratum influence', 'levelling', 'convergence', 'L1 influence on L2', and 'L2 influence on L1'. The model of Code Copying includes all kinds of linguistic copying and allows a coherent description of different ways of contact-induced influence, changes and developments. The phenomena produced in contact-induced processes are in fact essentially similar and should be treated in one and the same paradigm. The author's keen interest in linguistic variation has led to this in-depth investigation of language contact.

For fundamental questions of code copying see Johanson (1975b, 1991b, 1992, 1993b, 1997a, 1998c, 1999a, 1999b, 2000a, 2000b, 2002a, 2002b, 2002c, 2005a, 2005b, 2008a, 2008b, 2013a, 2013b, 2014a, 2014b, 2021, 2022), and Johanson & Csató (2022), Johanson & Robbeets (2012). The framework is summarized in Johanson (2002a, 2002c). Several different frameworks for dealing with contact-linguistic issues have been presented; see, for example, Ross (2001, 2005^2), Van Coetsem (2000), and Matras (2009). These will not be discussed here.

The study of contact languages should focus on the specific historical circumstances under which codes have arisen, changed, and vanished. The determinative factors are, as will be seen, whether copied items are 'taken over' or 'carried over', if their codes are superstrata, substrata, or adstrata, and whether they appear as primary codes or secondary codes.

2   Basic Code and Model Code

Code copying implies that features of a Model Code, also called Donor Code, are inserted into a Basic Code, also called Recipient Code. Copies of units and structures of a Model Code, e.g. English, are inserted into a Basic Code, e.g. German. Code is used in sociolinguistics as a cover term for a language or a variety of a language and is employed here as a non-technical term. Copying means imitation of one code by another. Copying processes, in which languages have been involved, have affected various linguistic subsystems such as lexicon, morphology, sound systems, prosodic features, and syntax.

3 Take-over and Carry-over Copying

There is a fundamental difference between 'take-over' copying and 'carry-over' copying. Speakers have taken over copies from a secondary code into their own primary code. They have carried over copies from their own primary code into their variety of a secondary code.

Take-over means that speakers of a primary code (L1), e.g. German, take over copies from a secondary code (L2), e.g. English. The primary code is then the Basic Code into which a copy of the English lexical item accommodated to German phonology is inserted, e.g. *lajf* 'live', e.g. broadcasting.

Take-over copying typically occurs in asymmetrical contact situations when speakers of a dominated language take over copies from a dominant language.

Carry-over means that speakers insert copies from their primary code into their own variety of a secondary code, e.g. when German speakers use their English with copies from German. The secondary code is then the Basic Code. An example is when German speakers use *also* 'thus' to introduce utterances in English: *Alzo, I told him ...* 'Thus, I told him ...'

The results of copying may imply that
- a new feature is added to the Basic Code, e.g. the category of dual is introduced into a language
- a Basic Code feature is replaced by a Model Code feature, e.g. Tajik copies of Turkic evidential verb forms
- a Basic Code feature is retained, assuming modified functions, e.g. when the Karaim suffixed postposition {-BA} 'with' acquires the syntactic function of the Russian instrumental case.

Certain contact situations have led to 'code shift', which means that speakers have shifted from their primary code to a secondary code. For instance, many speakers of Swedish in Australia have shifted to English.

4 Code Switching and Code Mixing

A different phenomenon, common in contact settings, typically in the speech of bilinguals, is 'code alternation', mostly called 'code switching'. It is the alternating use of two or more codes within one flow of discourse or stretch of conversation. 'Code mixing', or, in Muyskin's terminology, 'insertional code switching' (Muyskin 2000), occurs when a speaker inserts a word or a phrase from a model language into his / her frame language, for instance when he / she is unable to remember a correct term, but can recall it in a different language. Code switching and code mixing are radically different, and this terminology will not be used in this volume.

5 Global and Selective Copying

The framework applied here distinguishes between 'global copying' and 'selective copying'.

In cases of global copying, units of a Model Code, i.e. a phone, a phone sequence, a free or bound morpheme, or a morpheme sequence, is copied as an entire global block of material, semantic, combinational, and frequential properties; see Figure 1. The items, i.e. free and bound morphemes or morpheme sequences, are global blocks of properties. Globally copied lexical units are words and phrases. This is a kind of copying that code users themselves are generally most aware of, e.g. in the following Turkish sentence, a global copy of the German word *Bahnhof* 'railway station' is used with a Turkish case marker in (1).

(1) Global copy in Germany Turkish
 Model Code: Bahnhof
 ⇓
 Basic Code: ‹Banhof-a   gid-iyor-um.›
              station-DAT go-INTRA-1SG
              'I go to the railway station.'

It is the German word *Bahnhof* 'railway station' that is globally copied. The distributional properties, phonological, phonetic, supra-segmental features, the linear position, and the morphological properties of the copy have been accommodated to the Turkish frame.

In cases of selective copying, individual material, semantic, combinational, or frequential properties are chosen selectively and copied onto corresponding units of the Basic Code. A material copy is, for example, the use of retroflex [ʈ] occurring in the speech of some Hungarians in Norway, who pronounce the Hungarian word *kert* 'garden' as [kɛʈʰ].

(2) Selective material copy in Norway Hungarian
Model Code: Norwegian reftroflex   *ṭ*   e.g. *kort* 'short' [kʰoṭʰ]
⇓
Basic Code: Norway Hungarian   *rt > ṭ*   e.g. *kert* 'garden' [kɛṭʰ]

Selective grammatical copying means that copies of grammatical markers and patterns of a Model Code are inserted into the morphosyntactic frame of a Basic Code. The speaker choses an item in a Model Code and copies one or more of its properties onto a Basic-Code item, which is assessed as a more or less close equivalent of the model. Selectively copied combinational patterns are word structures, phrase, clause, sentence structures, ordering patterns, phonological structures, prosodic patterns, loan translations, etc. One example is the changed word order of possessive constructions in Karaim, which has been copied from Slavic. See the copied order (3b) instead of the canonical Turkic order (3a).

(3) Selective combinational copy in Northwest Karaim
Model Code: possessed +   possessor
                                         ot'ets   *Kariny*
                                         father   Karina's
                                                        ⇓
Basic Code: Copy:
a. possessor +   possessed >   b. possessed +   possessor
   Karina-nïn *ata-sï*   *ata-sï*   *Karina'nïn*
   Karina-GEN   father-POSS3SG   father-POSS3SG   Karina-GEN

A selective semantic copy is, for instance, the following. The meaning of English *iPad* has been copied onto the Swedish word *padda* 'toad', because of the phonetic similarity.

(4) Selective copy of a semantic feature
Model Code: iPad
⇓
Basic Code: *padda* 'toad' >   Copy: *padda* 'toad', 'iPad'

The Swedish word *padda* has become ambiguous as in the following sentence: *Min padda startar inte* 'My iPad/toad does not start'.

Selectively copied lexical units are lexical and phraseological copies, e.g. English *to up-date* is selectively copied as Swedish *att upp-datera* 'to up-date'.

Selectively copied frequential properties cause changes in frequency patterns, leading to increased or decreased occurrence of a given element. Turks speaking English frequently use *obviously* to render an evidential meaning that often occur in Turkish speech. This is a carry-over copy of the Turkish habit to express evidentiality. On the other hand the frequency of the Turkish evidential markers {-mIş} and {-(y)mIş}, in Germany Turkish is decreasing (Karakoç & Herkenrath 2019).

Semantic, combinational, and frequential properties are copied onto Basic Code elements, without accompanying any material properties. See Chapter 3.

Copying of semantic and combinational properties is traditionally referred to as 'grammatical calquing', 'loan semantics', 'loan translation', 'loan syntax', 'structural borrowing', 'grammatical replication', 'loanshift', 'indirect morphosyntactic diffusion', etc.

6 The Contact Globe

Many examples of different types of copying will be given in this volume. The phenomena mentioned can be illustrated by Figure 1. Its left side shows a whole 'globe' of material, semantic, combinational, and frequential properties. Its right side shows loose parts of a corresponding 'globe', i.e. selected material, semantic, combinational, and frequential properties.

Material properties are, for instance, sound types or intonational patterns, e.g. the copy of Arabic glottal stop in certain Turkish dialects. Semantic properties are, for instance, lexical or grammatical meanings, e.g. the use of Turkish ‹yıldız› 'star' with the meaning 'movie star'. Combinational properties include word order, e.g. Gagauz SVO basic word order copied from non-Turkic contact languages. A type of copying, often neglected, is copying of frequential properties, which manifests itself in increase or decrease in the frequency of use. As a result, an element or pattern may gain ground and become less marked, or it may lose ground and become more marked.

7 The Order of Influence

The order of contact-induced influence is not always clearly given. In general, global copying precedes selective copying. Global material copies appear before selective material copies. Global lexical copies emerge prior to globally copied bound morphemes. Globally copied phones as part of copies precede phones selectively copied onto units of the Basic Code.

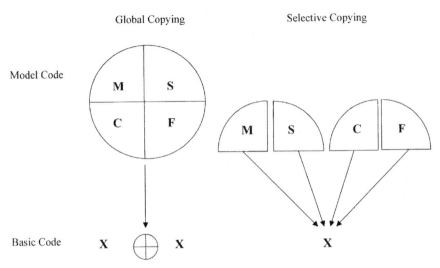

FIGURE 1   The contact globe
Legend:
M   material properties (substance)
S   semantic-pragmatic (meaning) properties
C   combinational properties (in word structure and syntax)
F   frequential properties
x   elements of a Basic Code

8   Copying Is a Creative Act

A copy is never identical to its original, i.e. it is not 'borrowed'. Copying creates something new. The copy is always adjusted to the receiving system, the Basic Code, and further developed there. For instance, Turkish globally copied the Arabic word ‹kırmızı› 'red' in addition to cognate ‹kızıl› 'red'. This has resulted in a semantic split between two types of red color. A language is an economical system, which would never accept taking over various foreign elements and putting them into another code as in a lumber room. Copying is both an act of imitation and a creative act. Copies are never imported goods, not even when the codes in contact are typologically similar. The result of copying is never borrowed, taken over, transferred, or imported, but it is always just a copy, and never the original. Copying leads to morphosyntactic convergence of the interacting codes, but not to the identity of a model and its copy. The copies are inserted into a morphosyntactic clause frame and are necessarily accommodated to it. Copies are always adapted to the system of the Basic Code and subject to its internal processes. Corresponding elements of the Basic Code may either be replaced by the copies or retained, fulfilling similar or different functions. It is important to note that through copying the frame changes gradually.

9 Attractiveness

The reason for Code Copying is mostly the wish to emulate elements of culturally or politically prestigious Model Codes. There may be a need to fill gaps, particularly in the lexicon. About different motivations for borrowing including the role of prestige and gap see, for example, Matras (2009: 149–153). Matras also emphasizes the importance of functional-communicative factors: "Underlining all the different motivations for borrowing is the bilingual's need to negotiate a complex repertoire of linguistic structure and to balance effectiveness and precision of expression again the social demand on complying with the norm to select only context-appriopriate structures" (p. 152).

The degree of copiability is determined by both social and structural factors, but certain structural properties may also play a decisive role. Some properties have proven 'attractive' for copying. Easily recognizable, straightforward relationships between content and expression are considered especially attractive. According to Slobin (1980), language learners prefer 'metaphorical transparency' between meaning and form as well as 1:1 relationship between linguistic forms and semantic configurations ('mapping transparency'). Copying seems to be guided by similar principles. Stolz demonstrates, for example, the high degree of copiability of a free, frequently used morpheme, the function word *allora* 'then, at that time', 'thus', 'therefore' (2007). This function word has been copied from Italian into a number of languages spolen in Italy and neighboring regions. Also bound morphemes can be attractive for copying. Especially clearly delineated elements of an agglutinative morphology are more attractive than the morphemes of inflectional languages, which are closely bound to their surroundings. Gardani gives an illustrative example of the attractiveness of nominal pural markers for borrowing, motivated by the agglutinative nature of this inflectional morpheme in many languages (2012: 93). Juxtaposition, where morpheme boundaries remain conspicuous, and relatively invariable allomorphy, that is relatively constant phonic shape of a morpheme in various environments, are attractive. For instance, the productivity and transparent form and semantics of many Turkic derivational suffixes have proved to be attractive and have been copied into many non-Turkic languages. The suffix {-CI}, deriving professions, has been copied, for instance, into Arabic such as ʿaragči 'drunkard' ← ʿarag 'aniseed brandy' (Procházka 2023). See a discussion of attractivity in relation to naturalness and markedness in Johanson (2002c: 41–43).

Attractive structures have often been sufficient to trigger copying. But strong social pressure has also led to copying of less attractive structures. If an element has been copied, it implies either that it has been attractive or that the social influence of the Model Code has been sufficient. Both factors may of course have been at work.

10 Contact Processes

The following processes have occurred in linguistic contact histories:
- Speakers of Basic Codes have *taken over* copies from Model Codes.
- Speakers of Basic Codes have *carried over* copies to Model Codes.
- Speakers of Basic Codes have *shifted* to Model Codes.

11 Extremely High Levels of Copying

Languages may go very far in copying, changing their original profile through massive contact influence. Some languages have thus acquired traits that appear to be typologically inconsistent with their basic structures. In cases of extremely strong copying, the only indigenous units left in a clause may be a few grammatical markers, pronouns, or derivational and inflectional suffixes. With respect to Turkic, Ottoman texts are well known examples of this in their use of Arabic-Persian elements. However, excessive copying has not caused languages to mutate into the codes they have copied from, thus shifting their genealogical affiliation; see Chapter 9.

Excessive copying has not caused one code to be absorbed by another. Quantitative criteria are not decisive for the assignment of the role of the Basic Code. Contact histories show examples of close intertwining of literary languages (Johanson 2013a). But they do not show fusion of the contact codes into 'hybrid languages' in any genealogical sense. Even the most high-copying texts cannot possibly be mistaken for belonging to a model text. Codes have not died for structural reasons, overwhelmed by foreign elements, suffering from 'structuritis' with lethal effects (Johanson 2002b). The reasons for language death and language shift have always been of social nature. Languages die when they are no longer handed down to new generations. The use of socially strong codes in asymmetrical settings tends to threaten the weaker codes, reducing their functional domains and thus marginalizing them. This has led to decreased maintenance efforts, declining linguistic competence, and finally to shift to the stronger code. Copying and shift have occurred in different dominance situations, under various sociocultural and socioeconomic conditions. Smaller languages have often been exposed to contact influence. Varieties relatively isolated from related standard languages and far from normative centers have proven particularly susceptible to contact-induced changes. Certain geographical areas have proven especially favorable to establishing contacts. Communication channels, e.g. trade routes, have been crucial for the spread of copied features. Modern media have highly facilitated contact-induced influence across borders.

12   Historical Stratification

In analyses of the circumstances under which codes have arisen, layers of historical stratification involving take-over and carry-over copying can be detected. The following strata may be distinguished:
– Superstrata, overlying layers, results of influence of codes more dominant than their contact codes.
– Substrata, underlying layers, results of influence of codes less dominant than their contact codes.
– Adstrata, adjacent layers, results of influence of codes of about equal dominance.
Superstrata and substrata raise important questions of code shift and code replacement. It is a frequent situation that a *local* code is used in a certain territory and that an *intrusive* foreign code intrudes through immigration. The intrusive code may exert superstratal influence on the local code. This is possible even if the local code is adopted by the immigrants. If, alternatively, the intrusive code persists and replaces the local code, it may be subject to substratal influence through carry-over copying of vocabulary and structural features. This is comparable to cases in which extinct European languages have left remnants in the languages that later have supplanted them. Examples are the old Celtic language Gaulish in the supplanting language French and the North Germanic Norn language in the modern Scots dialects of the Shetland and Orkney Islands. In cases of multiple substrata, the actual influence of each individual code is mostly difficult to determine. Substratal and superstratal influence cannot be distinguished, if the closest relatives of the influencing code are since long extinct. Questions concerning migration and political expansion are thus important for the contact history of languages. Political expansion has

sometimes led to linguistic expansion, but sometimes it has not. Relevant questions are: How did the speakers enter a given contact area? Did local speakers copy from the incoming codes, or did the incoming groups copy from the local codes? In the case of code shift, which group shifted? The strength of the migratory populations in cases of invasion and colonization is of high importance. There have been massive migratory movements, in which the incoming groups were numerically superior to the local populations. But there have also been minor movements of relatively small incoming élites, who, however, imposed their codes on larger existing populations.

Knowledge about substrata may help understand unattested prehistorical situations. Linguists work on methods for determining the effects of substratum influence in reconstructed languages by refining the concepts of determining substratum influence on the basis of recently attested or historically attested language shift situations. They apply the available methods to case studies of language shift in linguistic prehistory. Germanic, in its earliest form, may have been influenced by a non-Indo-European language. Roughly a third of Proto-Germanic lexical items have come from a non-Indo-European substratum. In controversial hypotheses on the creation of Indo-European protolanguages in northern Europe, it has been argued that the pre-Germanic substratum was of Uralic origin. Other researchers argue that the proto-Germans encountered a non-Indo-European speaking people and just copied many features from their language.

Substratal relationships are most interesting. Substratal carry-over is found in Gaulish or Basque elements in Western Romance. Gaulish has disappeared, but remnants of its vocabulary survive in French words and place-names. An Irish substratum is found in English, where carry-over has led to shifts and substratum influence. The Germanic substratum hypothesis is an attempt to explain the distinctive nature of Germanic in the Indo-European family.

Adstrata involve mutual copying between codes of about equal rank. Spanish and Portuguese, for example, have an Arabic adstratum. French and Dutch in Belgium are adstrata with roughly the same status.

Of the larger and smaller immigrant groups, e.g. in the USA, some give up their language after a generation or two, while others persistently retain it. The extinction of a language is often accompanied by pidginization. The harbingers include the dissolution and reduction of linguistic structures as well as a growing number of "semi-speakers".

1.3 Distinguishing Carry-over and Take-over Copying

Take-over copying is an intense form of contact. Languages that were more stable were weakly affected. Those that were less stable were strongly affected.

Effects of copying depend on the degree of affinity between the participant codes. The question is whether affinity can be defined as genealogical relatedness. The Uyghur substratum consists of genealogically unrelated Indo-European languages. The Uzbek and Azeri substrata consist of genealogically unrelated Persian varieties. The Chuvash substratum consists of genealogically unrelated Finnic, close to present-day Mari. The Yakut substratum is Tungusic, a language possibly related to Turkic. The influence of the non-related languages has led to phonological anomalies, in Chuvash even to a confusing phonology; see 1.14.

Carry-over copying in inflectional systems seems to be extremely rare between unrelated languages. But Yakut undoubtedly shows traces of a Tungusic substratum in its inflectional system, which might be seen as arguments in favor of genealogical relatedness of the languages. Yakut has two imperfects. The first Yakut imperfect is formed according to the pattern aorist stem + copula 'was', e.g. *Bar-ar ä-ti-m* 'I went', which corresponds to the norm in Turkic. A second imperfect has the pattern aorist stem + person-number agreement marker of the possessive type, e.g. 1SG *Bar-ar-ïm* 'I went'. The latter imperfect lacks a preterite marker. This is highly remarkable for Turkic. It can, however, be explained as a Tungusic copy (Johanson 2014b).

See also another example. Yakut converbs provided with subject person-number agreement markers represent another interesting case. Evenki possesses converbs provided with personal markers, part of a switch-reference system of marking different-subject constructions. Speakers of Evenki have partly carried over this feature to Yakut, changing the combinatory properties of Yakut converbs with respect to personal markers. However, while Evenki uses suffixes of a possessive type, Yakut uses suffixes of a pronominal type. This has led to claims that Evenki influence has not played any role in the development of person-marked converbs in Yakut (Pakendorf 2007: 7–14). But considered from the point of view of the code-copying framework, providing converbs with person markers is surely a combinatory copy carried over from the Evenki substratum. The possessive suffixes were replaced by suffixes of the pronominal kind, which were already common in the system. This development represents an innovation. Speakers of Evenki carried over these forms as selective copies and adapted them to the receiving system of Yakut.

Local non-Turkic codes have been abandoned in favor of intrusive immigrant Turkic codes but they have caused substrata of carry-over copying. Carry-over of lexical elements has been limited, but there are changes in grammatical structures. Even inflectional morphemes have been carried over. The major effects of carry-over copying are found in the phonology, i.e. sound changes due to inherited articulation habits. See Pakendorf (2014) on paradigm copying in Tungusic.

Codes of Turkicized groups represent the results of efforts to pronounce Turkic sounds. Though nearly all Turkic languages show systematic sound correspondences within their genealogical family, carry-over copying has led to irregularities in some cases. Minority groups rarely copy over lexicon. This would not be understood by the majority. If the Model Codes are unrelated to Turkic codes, phonology becomes discrepant. Umlaut is certainly not an attractive feature to take over. It can, however, be a result of carry-over in Uyghur. Minority groups shifting to Turkic have displayed their own characteristic pronunciation habits. On the pronunciation of Turkish by minorities in Turkey, see Kowalski (1934: 993).

Karachay-Balkar, spoken in the Caucasus area, is affected by lexical take-over copying and displays a relatively normal Turkic morphology and syntax. Some dialects, however, exhibit a Caucasian phonological substratum involving, for instance, ejective consonants. Karachay-Balkar has strong ejectives *p', t', k', k̦', č'* beyond the prime syllable and glottalic egressive consonants, e.g. *ärth-t'ä* 'in the morning'.

The degree of bilingualism and plurilingualism in older speaker communities is impossible to judge on. Multiple model languages may have resulted in homogeneity. Codes may be subject to limited or extensive copying, determined by social circumstances and attitudes. Differences can be observed in the extent and degree of copying. Turkic communities have always been ready to mix socially with other groups. Nomadic groups have had a great freedom to modify their codes.

These observations can be compared with other data. Some South Siberian varieties exhibit words of Yeniseic origin as a result of substratum influence. Slavic substrata are found in Balkan Turkish. Some South Siberian varieties exhibit Yeniseic phonological substratum influence. Greek substrata are found in several Turkic varieties, e.g. in the Black Sea dialects of Trabzon and Rize, probably also in Southwest Karaim.

The Romani variety spoken in the Athenian suburb Ajia Varvara, described by Igla (1996), is an example of unique carry-over influence. Turkish inflected verb forms have been carried over to a Romani code. Before settling in Greece, this group had lived in Turkey as bilingual speakers of Romani and Turkish. Their Romani code includes copies of verbs carried over from Turkish with preserved inflectional aspectual and personal markers in the present and past tense paradigms, e.g. *Calus-ur-um* 'I work' copied from *Čališ-ïr-ïm*.

The inflected forms were retained even several generations after emigration from Turkey and loss of competence in Turkish. The number of verbs conjugated in this way remained small like in Crimean Romani, which was influenced by another Turkic language, Crimean Tatar (cf. Matras 2009: 184). My framework accounts for the exceptional phenomenon in Ajia Varvara, to which there is no other explanation. The Komotini Romani, compared to Pomak by Adamou (2010) has no relation to this case and will not be discussed here.

14 Example of Carry-over Copying: Linguistic Convergence in the Volga Area

The complex linguistic situation in the Middle-Volga region will be briefly reviewed here in order to exemplify intertwined historical carry-over and take-over processes. The Middle-Volga area is regarded to be a convergence area in which different languages of adjacent speech communities have developed increasingly more common properties and thus come to resemble each other to a considerable degree. Contact-induced processes are supposed to have led to phenomena typical of a linguistic area in the sense of a so-called Sprachbund.

The main protagonists in this drama belong to two language families, Finno-Ugric and Turkic. The modern languages Mari (Cheremis), Udmurt (Votyak), and Mordva represent the Finno-Ugric side. On the Turkic side we find Tatar, Bashkir, and Chuvash. Tatar and Bashkir are closely related Kipchak languages. Chuvash, the descendant of Volga Bulghar and the only living representative of the Bulghar branch of Turkic, deviates a good deal from other known kinds of Turkic. And there is, of course, a further protagonist, Russian, an Indo-European language that has dominated this area during the last centuries. A few more languages, Finno-Permic Komi (Komi-Zyryan), Samoyedic Nenets, and Mongolic Kalmyk are sometimes included into the relevant language complex, but will not be dealt with here.

Numerous details concerning the interaction of the languages are obscure. Thus, no simple answer can be given to the question how these languages acquired their shared features. To what extent are the observable similarities due to mutual, adstrata influence, to common substrata or to original typological affinities?

The similarities observed may have different backgrounds. Successful reconstructions largely depend upon correct analyses of the copying processes. The distinction between carry-over and take-over copying is of crucial importance. Both are unidirectional convergence phenomena of two different kinds. The example of the widespread phonological opposition between lax vowels vs. tense vowels can serve here to illustrate the problems and some possible arguments for gaining insights into the contact processes on the bases of linguistic data.

So-called reduced vowels, which form opposition with so-called full vowels, are claimed to be a shared feature of typological importance in the area. They are found in several languages, e.g. Kazan Tatar, Mishar Tatar, Mountain Bashkir, Lowland Bashkir, Chuvash, Mari, Moksha Mordva, and Khanty (Vogul), an Ob-Ugric language. As a rule, the full vowels are ordinary tense vowels, whereas reduced vowels are lax and centralized. Significant differences between the vowel systems of the languages in the area show us that some features may have developed as a result of take-over copying, whereas others can only be seen as products of carry-over.

The Middle Volga region has experienced a complex interplay of socially dominated and dominant codes. Social dominance relations between the codes can be indicators of what kind of copying process could have taken place. It is important to keep in mind that the sociolinguistic role of most of the codes involved has changed from dominant to dominated.

Certain conclusions can be drawn from historical data. They suggest various asymmetrical relations between sociolinguistically dominated or 'weak' codes and dominant or 'strong' codes, i.e. fluctuating dominance relations in the course of the long-term contacts in the area. The prehistory of some Turkic varieties of the area is likely to have involved changes due to abrupt reorganization processes, when various ethnic groups using different codes were brought together to coexist in new confederations and other mixed speech communities with new social networks.

Only a few facts can be mentioned here. The Finno-Ugric languages involved are regarded as autochthonic in the region. The first significant Turkic element, Bulghar-Turkic groups, entered in the 8th century and came to dominate various Finno-Ugric tribes, the ancestors of the Mari, Mordva and Udmurt. Two points are important for the linguistic development: First, the Bulghar-Turkic state was a strong and rich empire of high cultural prestige and with a socially dominant language. Secondly, up to the 13th century, Bulghar tribes seem to have assimilated several Finno-Ugric groups living among them. This scene changed in the 13th century with the Mongol invasion, the fall of the Bulghar state and the establishment of the Golden Horde with the result that Kipchak Turkic became much more important in the area. The population was largely Kipchakized, e.g. acquired the language that later developed into Tatar and Bashkir. The Kipchak Turks had a politically and economically dominating role and assimilated the ethnic minorities of the region. The picture is complicated through the migration of the speaker groups. Russian influence began at different times. Russian colonization and the settlement of Russian peasants in the north and northwest split up the linguistic regions. For example, the Chuvash left their country in the 17th century. Some came to inhabit the southern regions of today's Chuvashia, and other went eastwards and thus came into contact with Tatar and Bashkir groups.

Take-over copying has taken place from Bulghar Turkic into Finno-Ugric varieties. There is a considerable stock of Bulghar Turkic lexical copies in Mari. Udmurt and Mordva also have a large number of Bulghar Turkic lexical copies. It is important to note that they are typically words of material and social culture, as we would expect in the case of take-over copying from a prestigious code. Elements of the dominant Kipchak language were taken over in all languages of the area.

Carry-over copying must be reckoned with, i.e. convergent changes due to complex processes of ethnolinguistic assimilation in the area. Thus, early carry-over copying from Finno-Ugric languages into Bulghar Turkic, and also from Bulghar and Finno-Ugric into Kipchak Turkic is highly probable.

Chuvash and Mari present the most intriguing interactions. The contacts between them have been extremely close, leading to a profound symbiosis. But the nature of their mutual copying processes is still far from clear. The direction of copying is often problematic. It is difficult to identify shared features as copies from Mari into Chuvash or copies from Chuvash into Mari. The fact is that there is a large scale of carry-over copying of Mari elements into Chuvash as against the take-over of Chuvash elements in Mari. This would imply that the Finno-Ugric influence on Chuvash is essentially a substratum influence due to assimilation of segments of a local Finno-Ugric population by Bulghar-Turkic speaking immigrants. The Finno-Ugric groups carried over features of their Basic Code on the variety of Bulghar Turkic.

This substratum influence in Chuvash is so strong that Chuvash was long mistaken for a Finno-Ugric language or a Turkicized Finno-Ugric language.

How can we distinguish between carry-over and take-over lexical copies? It may be enough to state here that possible semantic constraints on lexical copying are likely to differ between carry-over and take-over copying. In cases of take-over copying, speakers naturally tend to copy words that reflect the very aspects by which the culture of the dominant code is dominant. In cases of carry-over, speakers prefer the basic vocabulary of semantic domains left untouched by these aspects. Typically, Mari lexical copies in Chuvash are not items reflecting a prestigious social or material culture, but include basic everyday vocabulary such as *kïtkï* 'ant', *lïk* 'corner', *lïm* 'dew', 'moisture', *lïp* 'lukewarm', and *mïlke* 'shadow'.

As an example of selective copying, let us take a brief look at the phenomenon of lax vowels. A comparison of the Volga-Kipchak and the Chuvash vowel systems may demonstrate the difference between take-over and carry over copying of phonological features. In Volga-Kipchak a vowel shift has taken place. The old mid front vowels *e* and *ö* rise to *i* and *ü* and the old high vowels *i* and *ü* become lax *i̠* and *ü̠*. The old mid back vowel *o* becomes *u*, and *u* becomes lax *u̠*, whereas the old high back vowel *ï* becomes lax *ï̠*. The Turkic etymological relations are preserved, which means that there are regular correspondences between Tatar and other Common Turkic languages.

(5) Regular Tatar and Common Turkic correspondences (Berta 1989)

	Tatar	corresponding to	**Common Turkic**
'meat'	*it*		*et*
'to see'	*kür-*		*kör-*
'way'	*yul*		*yol*
'to know'	*bi̠l-*		*bil-*
'ashes'	*kül*		*kül*
'winter'	*ki̠š*		*kiš*
'worm'	*ku̠rt*		*kurt*

Volga Kipchak preserved the distinctions by analogous, though materially different phonetic means. Phonological confusion was avoided. Old phonemes left their slots, but their neighbors moved in after them. The chain reaction gradually influenced the whole system in a clear-cut way: the old correlation, so essential in Turkic, was now reinterpreted and expressed by means of tense and lax vowels. The etymological relations largely remained. Thus, the Volga Kipchak system is clearly motivated by internal principles of Turkic phonology. The material copy of lax vowels seems to be the result of take-over, a regional feature.

The situation is different in Chuvash. The Chuvash deviation from the normal Turkic vowel system is very different from those in Tatar and Bashkir. Chuvash has also tense and lax vowels. But the new system does not mirror the oppositions defining the earlier vowel system generally assumed for Turkic. If the latter was really the starting point for the Chuvash development, this development has not been systematic in the way observed in practically all other Turkic languages. The old distinctions high vs. non-high has not been preserved; and it has not been replaced by any analogous distinction. The tense vs. lax opposition does not serve the same phonological purpose as in Volga Kipchak.

The diachronic transparency is blurred; the etymological connections are broken. The problem of coinciding old high and non-high vowels has become unimportant, the whole system being reorganized regardless of old correlations.

Chuvash displays similar disloyalty with respect to old front vs. back relations. Many Turkic primary stems that are either front or back in a rather constant way from language to language are subject to class shift in Chuvash. There is thus a further dimension in which diachronic relations are disturbed and etymological connections blurred. See some examples with modern Common Turkic equivalents in (1).

(6)   Chuvash and Common Turkic correspondences

	Chuvash	corresponding to	Common Turkic
'interior'	i̮š		ič
'to drink'	i̮ś-		ič
'day'	kun		kün
'to laugh'	kul-		kül-
'ashes'	ki̮l		kül
'girl'	χir		ḳïz
'to hold'	tüt-		tut-
'ice'	pi̮r		buz
'to see'	kur-		kör-
'to die'	vil-		öl-
'root'	ki̮k		kök
'to put'	χur-		ḳoy-
'nine'	ti̮χi̮r		toḳuz

The comparison with Volga Kipchak is highly revealing. The vowel shifts found in Volga Kipchak are regional phenomena that are also observable in Finno-Ugric languages of the area. The deviations in Chuvash can only be explained by carry-over copying from Finno-Ugric. This means that the speakers of ancient Mari, and probably also Permic, carried over their articulation habits into their variety of Volga Bulghar. The phonological word structure of Turkic was alien to those speakers. Thus, the tense vs. lax features were preserved or reorganized under Finno-Ugric substrate influence, i.e. distributed according to the position in the word and to non-Turkic patters. Even if the tense vs. lax opposition originates in Volga Bulghar, these specific realizations seem to be the effects of Finno-Ugric carry-over.

CHAPTER 2

Global Copies

Most global copies are lexical items and phrases. Global copies of bound morphemes are less frequent, but occurs as the following examples demonstrate.

Bulgarian copies from Turkic. Bulgarian was for almost five centuries heavily influenced by Ottoman Turkish. Turkish words including, e.g., the nominal derivational suffix {-lIK} were globally copied, e.g. *avǰi-lăk* 'huntsman-ship', 'hunting' ← *avǰija* < *av* 'hunt(ing)' ⇐ Turkish *av*. Such copied suffixes could be combined with stems of Slavic origin, e.g. *bogat-lăk* 'richness' < *bogat* 'rich' and became productive derivational suffixes in Bulgarian.

Another example is the global copy of the Persian comparative suffix {-tar} used in addition to the native Turkic comparative suffix {-rAk} in Irano-Turkic, e.g. *böwüχ-tär* 'bigger' ← *böwüχ* 'big'. Some Irano-Turkic varieties display copies of the Persian suffix {-i}, which marks Persian nominals for indefiniteness, e.g. *keta:b-i* 'a book'. Turkic lacks an equivalent native marker but possesses the indefinite article *bir*, corresponding to Persian *yek*. In Azeri the suffix only occurs as part of complex copies. In Khalaj, however, it is copied globally as such and also added to native items. It can thus even be used, as in Persian, together with the indefinite article, e.g. Tebriz Azeri *bi: näfär-i:* 'a person' ⇐ Persian *yek … -i:*. It is thus an example of a mixed copy, a global copy within a copied combinational pattern (Kıral 2001, Johanson 1998b). Kashkay has copied an Iranian bound marker of definiteness in the form of the enclitic pronominal {-(y)aki}, which marks familiarity in Kashkay, e.g. (7). See Dolatkhah et al. (2016), Soper (1987).

(7) Kashkay copy of an Iranian enclitic marker
 Ušay-akï   sähär-änčä   aylä-di.
 child-YAKI until.morning cry-PAST3SG
 'The child (we are talking about) cried until morning.'

Many Irano-Turkic varieties display complex global copies whose originals are lexeme combinations. Some are formed with the Persian *iza:fat* relator {-(y)e}, which marks head-dependent relations in nominal phrases. Copies of combinations of nouns with other nouns, adjectives or numerals are, like simple copies, provided with the necessary Turkic morphosyntactic markers. For instance, Tebriz Azeri *eyd-e nowru:z-da* 'at the New Year's feast' include the Turkic locative suffix. This shows that copies are accommodated to the frame of the copying Turkic Basic Code. Non-final members of such complexes may even carry copies of Persian plural suffixes, e.g. Khorasan Turkic *a:dämʰa:-ye fa:yir* 'poor people', in which *a:dämʰa:* is a plural form.

Examples of copied free grammatical elements are, for instance, Persian prepositions. Copied Persian prepositions normally take Turkic case morphology to be able to occur adverbially. The Persian preposition *dar* 'in' is copied into Tebriz Azeri, but it must be used together with the native locative case suffix, e.g. *där täbiät-ta* 'in nature' ⇐ Persian *dar tabiyat*. Thus, a native relator, i.e. a Turkic case suffix, is required for the syntactic anchoring. The prepositive Persian copies specify the semantic content of the relation signaled, whereas the native case markers or postpositions take over the syntactic anchoring.

There are also globally copied complex items of a grammatical nature: complexes that have already been grammaticalized to relators in the original code. Interestingly enough, such items are more susceptible to global copying than simple grammatical items. There are, for instance, complex prepositional phrases that are globally copied as such. A frequent Persian pattern is: simple preposition + nominal core + *iza:fat* marker. The simple preposition can be such as *dar* 'in', *az* 'from', *be* 'to'. A number of such constructions have been globally copied into various Turkic languages and, for instance, Irano-Turkic varieties display such complex copies.

(8) Irano-Turkic copies of Persian simple preposition + nominal core + iza:fat marker
    'on the part of'   *az täräf-e*   + Turkic dative suffix
    'concerning'   *märbut be*   + Turkic dative suffix
    'concerning'   *där båre-ye*   + Turkic ablative suffix, e.g. *där båre-ye ušaχ-lïy-ïnan* 'concerning (my) childhood'

An Uzbek example is *bad az nån-da* 'after the meal' ⇐ Persian *baʔd az* 'after', where {-da} is the Uzbek locative. Khalaj may even use an additional synonymous Turkic postposition, *soy* 'after', which normally requires the Turkic ablative suffix.

(9) Khalaj
    bäd äz äk:i kün-dä   soy
    after two day-ABL after
    'after two days'

But remarkably enough, Khalaj *bäd äz* can also dispense with a native anchor, e.g. *bäd äz män* 'after me'. This can also be the case in certain copied fixed expressions which may dispense with the Turkic anchoring morphology, e.g. *be här hål* 'in any case' ⇐ *be har ha:l*.

In Turkic, such copies are often used as clausal adjunctors (conjunctive adverbials), and some of the originals contain Persian demonstrative pronouns, see (10).

(10) Copied clausal adjunctors

	Irano-Turkic	⇐	Persian
'therefore'	*be hämin χåtir*		*be hamin xa:tir*
'in that case'	*där un surät*		*dar u:n surat*
'before this'	*gäbl äz in*		*qabl az i:n*
'after that'	*bäʔd äz un*		*baʔd az u:n*

For their use as causal junctors, see more in Johanson (1993c, 1996b).

CHAPTER 3

Selective Copies

1 Selective Copying of Material/Phonological Features

One type of selective copying is exclusively material and manifests itself as 'loan phonology'. Phonic aspects of units serve as models. Segments and patterns typical of the Model Code are copied onto units of the Basic Code. Distinct phonological structures are acquired by copying sounds, phonotactic patterns, and accent patterns of stress and pitch. The influence may lead to allophonic shift. West Rumelian Turkish has *o* instead of *ö* and *u* instead of *ü* as a result of Slavic influence, e.g. West Rumelian Turkish *dort* < Turkish ‹dört› 'four' and West Rumelian Turkish *uč* < Turkish ‹üç› 'three'. Eastern Black Sea Turkish dialects show a corresponding change under Greek influence, e.g. Eastern Black Sea Turkish *on* < Turkish ‹ön› 'front' and Eastern Black Sea Turkish *uč* < Turkish ‹üç› 'three'. The Irano-Turkic languages Khalaj and Kashkay have taken over delabialization of *ö* and *ü* from Persian, e.g. Khalaj *kin* 'day' < *kün*, *kez* 'eye' < *köz*. Turkish of Sweden and Norway has taken over the Swedish and Norwegian retroflex plosive [ʈ] after [r], e.g. [dœʈʰ] 'four' < Turkish ‹dört›.

Contact with non-Turkic languages can weaken the native phonotactic principle of syllabic harmony. In South Oghuz and Khorasan Turkic non-harmonic suffixes are often found, e.g. Azeri *elä-maχ* 'to do'. Khalaj has a weak harmony system, e.g. *Var-di-k* 'We went' instead of a harmonic form **Var-dï-k*, *Hač-ül-di* 'X opened (itself)' instead of a harmonic form **Hač-ül-dü*.

Turkic languages dominated by Slavic languages have copied palatalized consonants. An interesting example is Northwest Karaim, which has palatalized and non-palatalized varieties of all consonants. Their use, however, obeys the rules of Turkic syllabic harmony and does not reflect the functional and distributional patterns of palatalized consonants in the Model Codes. Palatalized consonants occur in front syllables together with front vowels and non-palatalized consonants occur in back syllable with back vowels, e.g. *K'el'!* 'Come!', *Kal!* 'Stay!'.

Material copies are often carried over from the speaker's primary language into his/her secondary language resulting in a 'foreign accent'. Hungarian speakers of Norwegian as a secondary language carry over their native phonotactic rules of regressive voice assimilation of adjacent consonants into their Norwegian, e.g. Norwegian spoken by Hungarians *fla:dbrø:* ⇐ Norwegian *fla:tbrø:* 'flatbread'.

2 Selective Copying of Semantic Features

Semantic copying causes changes in content. It refers to any kind of pattern copying, that is, copying of grammatical patterns, e.g. developing identical patterns of relative clauses, and also copying of semantic patterns, e.g. developing similar idioms and ways of saying things. The semantics of units of a Model Code is copied onto equivalent units of the Basic Code. This influence manifests itself as so-called 'loan semantics' and produces semantic calques and, as far as lexical units are concerned, 'loan translations'. Again, there is no identity between originals and copies, but differences at the denotative or connotative level due to adaptation to the semantic system of the Basic Code. Turkish in Germany tends to take over the meaning 'among' of the German preposition *unter* 'among' and copy it on the Turkish postposition ‹altında› which originally means 'under'.

In the lexicon of Irano-Turkic languages, there are numerous examples of semantic properties copied from Persian. Grammatical items are also affected. Properties of the Persian perfect, consisting of the perfect participle + copula, e.g. *Raft-e ast* 'X has gone', have been copied onto the Azeri item {-(y)Ib(di)}, which behaves as a typical postterminal with present relevance, e.g. *Ged-ib-di* 'X has gone'. In non-third persons, forms in {-mIš} are used, e.g. *Gel-miš-äm* 'I have come', without expressing the evidentiality typical of the Turkish postterminal {-mIš}, e.g. ‹Gel-miş-im› 'I have apparently come' (Johanson 1971: 280ff.). The fact that {-mIš} forms do not signal evidentiality in Irano-Turkic varieties seems to be due to Persian influence. See Karakoç & Herkenrath (2019) about the decline in the frequency of {-mIš} and {-(y)ImIš} in Turkish in Germany.

Properties of the Persian copula {-(y)e} and {-ast} 'is', 'exists' have been copied onto Turkic {-dIr}, so that the latter may also express existence in the sense of 'there is', which is normally taken care of by the adjective *var* 'existing'. See Karakoç (2009).

3 Selective Copying of Combinational Features

Combinational copying may create new placement patterns, phrase structure rules, rules for lexical subcategorization, valency patterns, and word-internal morphemic patterns. The rection of verbs of a Model Code may be copied onto equivalent verbs of the Basic Code.

Germany Turkish tends to use cases such as (11). See also Rehbein et al. (2009).

(11) Copying of case assignment in Germany Turkish
   a. Germany Turkish
      ‹Adam-ı   sor-du-m.›
      man-ACC ask-PAST-1SG
      'I asked the man.' with an accusative instead of a dative complement as in Standard Turkish ⇐ German *Ich fragte den Mann.*

   b. Standard Turkish
      ‹Adam-a   sor-du-m.›
      man-DAT ask-PAST-1SG
      'I asked the man.'

West Rumelian Turkish shows cases of dative-locative confusion, since its contact languages express 'motion toward' and 'location' by the same markers. Other combinational phenomena typical of the syntax of the model/donor code may be copied. Turkish in Germany shows cases such as *dört dost-lar-ım* 'my four friends', taken over from cases such as German *meine vier Freund-e* instead of the standard expression *dört dost-um*. The internal combinational pattern of a complex of the Model Code may be copied onto equivalent units of the Basic Code. Turkish of Germany uses cases such as *her ikinji hafta* 'every second week', taken over from *jede zweite Woche* instead of the standard expression ‹iki hafta-da bir› literally 'two week-in one'. See Backus (1996) on bilingual speech of Turkish immigrants in the Netherlands.

Word order changes may play an important role. Head-initial patterns may be copied onto head-final constructions, and vice versa. Dependents that are normally placed in front of or after their heads may become postpositive or prepositive, respectively.

For instance, West Rumelian Turkish exhibits orders as in *baba-si Ali-nin* 'Ali's father' with the components father + possessive suffix and *Ali* in the genitive instead of standard *Ali'nin baba-si*. It is taken over from Macedonian *tatko mu na Ali* or/and Albanian *babai i Aliut*.

Constituent order patterns are copied in Irano-Turkic, e.g. (12) (Johanson 1997b).

(12) Copying constituent order
   a. Tebriz Azeri
      bi suχ   adam
      a funny man
      'a funny man'

b. Turkish
   ‹komik bir insan›
   funny a   man
   'a funny man'

Tebriz Azeri has the order indefinite article + adjective attribute + head instead of the typical Turkic order adjective attribute + indefinite article + head as in Turkish.

The interrogative suffix {-mI}, which has no Persian equivalent, is mostly absent and replaced by a special intonational pattern in Irano-Turkic.

Several Irano-Turkic varieties exhibit possessive constructions in which the adjective *va:r* 'existent' takes over combinational properties of the Persian verb *dāštan* 'to have'. For instance, in the Khalaj expression (13).

(13) Khalaj
   Hat   va:r-um.
   horse existing-COP.1SG
   'I have a horse' ⟸ Persian *Asp dār-am*.

In this construction, the native element *var* 'existing' bears the subject-representant suffix—here for the first person singular—as a copy of the Persian inflected form of the verb *da:štan*. The native Turkic pattern is (14).

(14) Standard Turkish
   ‹At-ım   var.›
   horse-POSS1SG existing
   'I have a horse.'

In this construction, the possessed *at* 'horse' bears a possessive suffix representing the possessor (Karakoç 2019).

In most Irano-Turkic varieties, the suffix {-lIk} takes over properties of the Persian abstract suffix {-ī} in globally copied items, e.g. Azeri dialect *jävan-niχ* 'youth' ⟸ Persian *javān-ī*, Tebriz Azeri *åzåd-lïg* 'liberty' ⟸ Persian *āzād-ī*, *bädbäχ-ti-lïχ* 'bad luck' ⟸ Persian *badbax-tī*. In Khalaj, almost every use of the Persian {-ī} can be rendered by {-lUχ}.

Properties of Persian modal verb constructions expressing 'to want', 'to be able to', 'to have to' have been copied onto equivalent items of Irano-Turkic varieties, e.g. *eliyä bil-* 'to be able to' + optative ⟸ Persian *tavānestan* + subjunctive, *gäräh* 'necessary' + optative ⟸ Persian *bāyad* 'necessary' + subjunctive. The construction *istä-* 'to want' + optative ⟸ Persian *xāstan* + subjunctive has ousted the native construction {-mAK} + *istä-*, e.g. (15).

(15) Kashkay
Is-ir-äm (ki) sän gäl-ä-ŋ biz-im äv-ä.
want-INTRA-1SG JUNCT you come-OPT-2SG we-GEN house-DAT
'I want (that) you come to our home'.

The complement clause of the predicate 'I want' is a postposed clause introduced by the junctor *ki* and contains the finite predicate *Gäl-ä-ŋ* 'May you come' in the optative (Dolatkhah 2022).

Combinational properties of the Persian infinitive are often copied onto the Southern Azeri verbal noun in {-mAK}, which may occur in genitive constructions such as (16).

(16) Southern Azeri
o ev-ün al-may-i ⇐ Persian *xarīdan-e ūn xūne*
that house-GEN purchase-VN-POSS3SG
'the purchase of that house'

4 Semantic-Combinational Copies

Semantic-combinational copies are very common. They are traditionally called 'calques' or, in the lexicon, 'loan translations'. Turkish in Nothwestern Europe shows cases such as *čorba ye-* 'to eat soup' instead of *čorba ič-* with the verb *ič-* 'to drink', according to German *zu essen* 'to eat' in *Suppe essen*, Swedish *äta* 'to eat' in *att äta soppa*, and Norwegian and Danish *spise* in *å spise suppe* and *at spise suppe*. Cases such as *piyano oyna-* 'to play the piano' are used instead of *piyano čal-*, with the verb *čal-* 'to strike', 'to knock', taken over from Swedish *att spela piano* or Danish *at spille klaver*. See more examples of semantic copying in Türker (2000).

4.1 *Postpositions Modelled on Prepositional Patterns*

There is a tendency in Irano-Turkic to turn copies of Persian prepositions into postpositions, e.g. by copying properties of *iza:fat* combinations onto Turkic possessive constructions. Turkic has declinable postpositions of the structure nominal core + possessive suffix + simple relator, corresponding to the Persian pattern simple preposition + nominal core + *iza:fat* relator. The nominal core is often a spatial noun such as *ič* 'interior' and *arka* 'back'. Given their special syntactic behavior, these postpositions are not simply members of normal possessive constructions, but constitute the particular word class of postpositions (Johanson 2021: 542–554).

The nominal cores can be global copies from prestigious contact languages, e.g. the nominal core of the Turkish postpositions ‹sebeb-i-yle› 'because of', ‹taraf-ın-dan› 'by', 'on the part of', ‹saye-sin-de› 'thanks to' are copies of Arabic-Persian models. Comparable patterns underlie prepositions such as English *because of* 'for the reason of'. Thus, postpositions such as Tebriz Azeri *mo:red-in-dä* 'with respect to' are modelled on patterns such as Persian *där mōrede*. Khalaj also exhibits postpositions of more reduced shape, e.g. *täräf* + dative 'towards', where only the nominal core ('side') of the Persian model is left. As is well known, complex junctors tend to undergo formal simplification in the course of their grammaticalization processes.

Complex prepositional phrases such as English *because of* 'by reason of', literally 'by cause of', have been taken over by many languages. German shows *in puncto* + genitive 'with respect to', literally 'in the point of', and Dutch *in termen van*, taken from English *in terms of*.

4.2 Combinational Copying in Clause Junction

Here the copying of foreign clause linking elements into Turkic will be considered. Clause junctors are connective units that represent products of different grammaticalization processes. They serve the function of clause linking, the use of two neighboring predications in the sentence or in the text by indicating content relations between them.

The essential difference between English or Russian and Turkic is that the embedding subordination in Turkic mainly occurs through bound junctors, for example through verbal nominal or converb suffixes such as {-sA} in *kel-sä* 'if X comes' (Johanson 1995).

Turkish free relators or function words, e.g. conjunctions, are taken over from Persian, Arabic, Slavic, and other languages, etc. ‹amma› 'but', ‹ve› 'and', ‹hem› 'and', ‹ki› 'that' (and other meanings), ‹zira› 'for' from Arabic-Persian, whereas in Turkic influenced by Slavic *i* 'and', *a* 'and', 'but', *no* 'but', *to* 'that, then' etc. are taken from Slavic. There are also global copies of bound relators. Dialects of Kurmanji have taken over {-se}, from the Turkish conditional copula ‹ise› 'if', 'when', e.g. *hat-se* 'if/when X comes' (Bulut 2006: 107).

Free junctors in the sense of English and Russian conjunctions are, specially in older stages of development, relatively infrequent in Turkic. Today Siberian Turkic languages as Kirghiz and also Kazakh still have only relatively weak systems of free conjunctions. The use of suffixed means of clause linking dominates. The asyndetic juxtaposition of clauses without any linking element is relatively frequent, e.g. (17).

(17) Turkish
‹Ali hasta. Gel-me-di.›
Ali sick come-NEG-PAST3SG
'Ali is sick. He has not come.'

Nevertheless, Turkic languages have copied certain conjunctions from their contact languages very early. The junctor *ki*, copied from Iranian, has the widest use. It is a connector of a very general kind with a wide extension of functions (Johanson 1975a[1991: 210–224]). In the Islamic Turkic languages, especially in Turkish, Azeri, Turkmen, Tatar, Bashkir, Uzbek and Uyghur, the majority of conjunctions is of Arabic-Persian origin. Even today's Turkish possesses almost exclusively copied free junctors such as ‹çünkü› 'for', and ‹eğer› 'if'.

Many Turkic languages have also globally or selectively copied Slavic conjunctions and relative items and use them productively. As for the languages of the Russian influence sphere, Russian Turcologists have spoken of an increase in the number of auxiliary words, in particular of conjunctions, of which there were remarkably few in the old language (Johanson 1997a).

The introduction of new types of junctors has contributed to the typological change in the area of clause combining and led to functional and formal convergence with the systems of clause linking in the respective dominant languages.

Free junctors, which represent copies of subordinative conjunctions, occur in different older and more recent Turkic languages. Still today they are typical for the languages that are most influenced by Iranian and Slavic. Minor Altaic languages that have developed under strong Russian influence tend to copy subordinated sentence type of the Russian kind (Comrie 1981: 85). Soviet Turcologists considered this influence specifically blessed. Through increased use of Russian subordinative means the grammar of those languages would be 'perfect', 'modernized', and 'normalized'. An example was the small South Siberian Turkic language Khakas that for understandable historical reasons displays no copied conjunctions from Arabic and Persian. It was self-evident that the further development of the Khakas written language would lead to more complexity of the syntax, specifically through use of free junctors (Baskakov 1975: 269).

It should, however, be noticed that copies of subordinative conjunctions were mostly used in a different way than in the model language. In many cases the Turkic junctors do not function as subjunctors but as conjunctors and adjunctors. In the imitations of Russian hypotaxis there are great differences in this regard between models and copies. Thus, for instance, the copied junctor *ki* does not subordinate clauses in Turkish (Johanson 1975a, 1991b).

Semantic and combinational features of foreign conjunctions have been selectively copied on native Turkic elements, namely on Turkic interrogative pronouns. This phenomenon is already documented in East Old Turkic (Gabain 1950: 189). Also in many later languages, for example in Balkan Turkic, such items often function as junctors, e.g. Gagauz *ani* 'that', *angi* 'which', *aniki* 'therewith', *ačan* 'when', *nečinki* 'because' (Menz 2001). A Gagauz example is (18).

(18) Gagauz
Da soram uže gör-er-im ani bit-ti on-nar-ïn
and later already see-INTRA-1SG that finish-PAST3SG they-GEN
para-lar-ï.
money-PL-POSS3
'And later I already notice that their money is finished.'

The complement clause 'that their money is finished' is introduced by the interrogative pronoun *ani* and its predicate is a finite verb form (Csató & Menz: 2018: 50).

There are many other types of syntactic combinational copying in Irano-Turkic varieties, for instance, in the area of clause junction. Head-initial Persian patterns tend to replace head-final patterns of the Turkic type. Combinational copying has led to new placement patterns. In all Turkic varieties under strong Persian influence, nonfinite clauses placed in front of their heads have largely been replaced by postposed clauses with finite morphology, formed according to Persian patterns. Most syntactic copying in the area of clause junction is mixed, the junctors being global copies of Persian models. See the Azeri example (19) of a postposed finite clause with an Azeri optative verb form and a global copy of the Iranian junctor *ki*.

(19) Azeri
a. *Arzu ed-ir-äm ki ḳayïd-a-sïnïz.*
wish-INTRA-1SG JUNCT return-OPT-2PL
'I wish you will return.'

b. *Istä-yir-äm ki gäl-sin.*
wish-INTRA-1SG JUNCT come-VOL3SG
'I want X to come.'

5 Selective Copying of Frequential Patterns

Frequential patterns of Model Code elements can be copied onto Basic Code elements, leading to increased or decreased use of the latter. Frequential copying may, in its initial, weak forms, violate pragmatic norms, while not leading to manifest linguistic change.

As noted above, language contact frequently results in over- or undermarking. Frequential copying may thus increase or decrease the use of anaphoric pronouns in 'pro-drop' codes (Johanson 1992: 254; 2002c: 110–111). See Brendemoen (1993) on the changed frequency of pronouns in Black Sea dialects.

The use of one linguistic option may increase at the expense of another option. This may mean increased use of plural markers in codes with restricted plural marking patterns. The use of an element may also decrease due to frequential copying. A two-way system of definite articles may, for example, lose ground in favor of a one-way system. Speakers of Dutch in Australia tend to copy combinational properties of the English definite article *the* onto the Dutch article *de*, gradually giving up the article *het* (Clyne 2003: 22, 31).

Frequential copying is a major factor in supporting constituent ordering patterns. Under the influence of an equivalent ordering pattern in the Model Code, frequential properties are copied onto existing patterns available in the Basic Code. An existing ordering pattern may thus be extended to new contexts and used more frequently. A pre-existing pattern may be overgeneralized, i.e. reinforced by frequential copying, while the frequency of use of an unsupported alternative diminishes accordingly. This reinforcement by analogy gives preference to features which the contact languages seem to have in common; Johanson (1992: 182–183, 215, 252, etc.; 2002c: 18, 61, 108, etc.).

Thus the resulting constituent ordering patterns are not really new. Only their frequency and their extended or narrowed contextual occurrence are new. This analysis corresponds to Heine's scenario of "word order change without word order change" (2006). After his overview and discussion of numerous data in various languages, Heine notes that he has "not come across a single case where speakers produced an entirely new word order" (2006: 19). This conclusion is perfectly in line with my understanding of frequential copying.

A simple example: The Basic Code may have the two alternative constituent order patterns, subject-object-verb *I you love* and subject-verb-object *I love you*. The last order may be acceptable, but more marked. The frequency of a Model Code pattern is copied onto the equivalent Basic Code subject-object-verb pattern *I love you*, i.e. onto the alternative order that matches the Model Code order. Due to this frequential copying, the pattern subject-verb-object is extended to new contexts and used more frequently. It may develop from a pragmatically marked pattern into a pragmatically unmarked pattern. The alternative pattern *I you love* may eventually be replaced by *I love you*, which is then the only pattern available. Alternatively, it may be retained, but assigned modified functions.

Heine notes that the word order changes dealt with by him concern processes of grammaticalization "that could in principle have happened as well *internally*, that is, without language contact; in other words, it is not possible to 'prove' that contact was a contributing factor" (2006: 20). I claim that a 'natural' or 'universal' tendency, e.g. towards analytic constructions as against synthetic constructions, can be more or less reinforced by frequential copying. A certain natural structure, which is already latently present in the Basic Code, can be strengthened through contact with a Model Code that possesses an equivalent structure. The introduction of the structure in the Basic Code is facilitated or accelerated through frequential copying. We must thus supplement the simple question 'copying or independent tendency?' by the further alternative 'or a natural tendency reinforced by the contact language?' (Johanson 1992: 278–279, 2002c: 142).

In Irano-Turkic varieties, Persian plural marking has induced a wider use of the Turkic plural suffix, namely on predicates occurring with collective nouns such as *märdom* 'people' (*constructio ad sensum*). However, the use of plural markers after certain quantifiers, e.g. Tebriz Azeri *čox adam-nar* 'many men', cf. Turkish ‹çok adam›, is basically an example of combinational copying. Persian influence has also led to a more frequent use of *vä* and *ki* as sentence-introducing items in the sense of 'and then', 'moreover'.

Frequential copying may effect the use of constituent ordering patterns. As in spoken Persian and Kurdish, adverbials of direction and purpose are often postposed, e.g. (20) and (21).

(20) Tebriz Azeri
    O ged-di   Teflis-ä.
    X go-PAST3SG Tiflis-DAT
    'X went to Tiflis' ⇐ Persian *U raft Teflis.*

(21) Tebriz Azeri
    Män otur-du-m   on-a   bax-may-a.
    I   sit-PAST-1SG X-DAT watch-VN-DAT
    'I sat down to watch it' ⇐ Persian *Man nešastam be didan-e u.*

SELECTIVE COPIES

This tendency is not observed in clauses embedded according to native Turkic rules, e.g. in the adverbial clause built with a converb (22).

(22) Tebriz Azeri
ev-ä ged-än-dä
home-DAT go-CONV
'when going home'

Spoken Persian often uses sentence-initial nominals in the so-called *nominativus pendens* which marks a sentence topic which is not necessarily referentially identical to the first actant (subject). The referent can be taken up again in the sentence with a properly case-marked anaphoric pronominal item in the proper syntactic position (Windfuhr 1979: 72–73). Irano-Turkic varieties often display similar initial sentence topics as in (23).

(23) Tebriz Azeri
Dädä-si vä:zi yaχši-y-di.
father-POSS3SG situation good-COP-PAST3SG
'As for his father, the situation was good.'

Such patterns are also observed in other Turkic languages, e.g. Ottoman Turkish. It seems appropriate to speak of frequential copying in this case.

5.1 *Frequential Copies in Clause Junction*

Certain Irano-Turkic clause-junction types are frequential properties of Persian originals. Their increased use means decreasing frequency of verbal nominals and converbs. Relative clauses with attributed verbal nominals are rare. Forms with the verbal nominal {-(y)An}, which are typical non-finite verb forms in Turkic relative clauses, are predominantly used as nouns. This corresponds to the restrictive use of the Persian present participle in {-ande}, which has lost many of its verbal properties and passed into the category of nouns. This tendency is observed in all Irano-Turkic varieties such as Azeri, Khorasan Turkic, and Khalaj.

The decreasing use of Turkic clause-combining techniques has led to a reduction of Turkic bound subjunctors. Tebriz Azeri has preserved the temporal junctors, case marked verbal nominals without or with a postposition such as {-yAn-dA} 'when', {-(y)An-nAn} *sora* 'after', and {-(y)An-nAn} *gabaχ* 'before'. Terminal and purposive junctors such as {-(y)An-A} *kimin* 'until' and {-mAG-A} 'in order to' are threatened by copies of Persian *ta inke*. Turkic causal subjunctors have been ousted by items such as *čün-ki* and *čon* ⇐ Persian.

The non-finite adverbial converb in {-(y)Ib} is seldom used in Irano-Turkic varieties, probably due to identification with the Persian perfect (Johanson 1988: 249).

6 Mixed Copies

Mixed copies consist of copied combinatory patterns with at least one Turkic native item. Besides complex global copies of the type *rūz be rūz* 'day by day' ⇐ Persian, many Turkic languages also have synonymous mixed copies such as *gün be gün* 'day by day'. In Irano-Turkic varieties, most phraseological verbs consisting of a nominal item and an auxiliary verb are mixed copies of Persian originals. The nominal item is copied globally, and the auxiliary is a Turkic verb, mostly *elä-* 'to do', 'to make' ⇐ Persian *kardan*, onto which combinational properties of the original are copied. See examples in (24).

(24) Mixed copies

	Tebriz Azeri	⇐ Persian
'to endeavor'	*täläs elä-*	*talās kardan*
'to phone'	*telefon vur-*	*telefon zadan*

Some variants are solid selective copies, containing both an equivalent Turkic nominal and a Turkic auxiliary, e.g. *sagal vur-* 'to shave' ~ *rīš vur-* ⇐ *rīš zadan*. Historically, they often represent a later stage of development than the mixed copies. While the *iza:fat* construction is normally not copied to be used with Turkic items, Khalaj offers examples that include one Turkic member, e.g. Khalaj *baluχ* 'village' in the expression (25).

(25) Khalaj
 baluχ-i diyär 'another village' ⇐ Persian *dih-i digar*

Mixed copies with a native item as first member are also possible in Tebriz Azeri, e.g. *balïy-e mäχsus* 'the particular fish', in which the word *balïy* 'fish' is native. The combinational properties of the construction are selectively copied, whereas the Persian word *mäχsus* 'particular' is globally copied.

Semantic and combinational properties of Persian grammatical items are sometimes copied onto Turkic units in order to use them analogously. Thus, the Turkic demonstrative pronouns *bu* 'this' and *o* 'that' may occur in mixed copies such as (26).

(26) Mixed copies

	Tebriz Azeri ⇐	Persian
'before this'	*gäbl äz bu*	*qabl az īn*
'after that'	*bäd äz o*	*ba'd az ūn*

Such adverbial copies may also be anchored syntactically by means of Turkic postpositions, e.g. *gäbl äz on-nan gabaχ* 'before that', *bä'd äz on-nan sora* 'after that'. Tebriz Azeri also uses *sora-dan k'i* 'after', a mixed copy of the Persian subjunctor *ba'd az inke*. This kind of selective copying seems to presuppose the existence of corresponding globally copied grammatical items.

6.1   Mixed Copies with Junctors

As we have stated, several copies of combinational patterns are in reality mixed copies. An extreme case is Khalaj *bi: sän* 'without you' with a global copy of a Persian preposition together with its combinational pattern added to the native pronoun 'you'. In all Irano-Turkic varieties, the preferred way of linking a dependent clause to its head by means of a junctor has been changed. Copies of Persian subordinated clauses are mostly finite postpositive predications with globally copied free junctors; see the parameters discussed in Johanson (1993c, 1996b). The postpositive relative clauses are usually marked with the junctor *ki* ⇐ Persian *ke*. Many copies of this versatile Persian relator do not behave as genuine subjunctors in the Turkic Basic Codes they are inserted to. They are often used as conjunctors, even if the original may be subordinative. The same is true of many other junctor copies.

On the other hand, there are obviously cases of genuine embedding of clauses introduced copies of Persian subjunctors. Such clauses differ considerably from corresponding structures in languages such as Turkish. For example, Irano-Turkic causal clauses marked with *čün-ki* or *čon* 'because' may precede the clauses they are in construction with. This is not possible with Turkish ‹çün-kü› clauses, which are not subordinated in the sense of being syntactically embedded.

The new combinational patterns involve changes in the position and nature of the junctors. The Turkic pattern predication + bound junctor is changed into free junctor + predication, e.g. *X come-when* > *when X comes*. Subjunctors mostly occur at the periphery of the dependent with which they form a constituent. They tend to stand behind a dependent that precedes the matrix predication, and in front of a dependent that follows it. Ordering patterns and subjunctor types are thus closely interconnected. Subjunctors cannot be copied into incongruous structures. That means that copies of Persian subjunctors cannot be inserted directly into Turkic frames to fill the slots of bound junctors such as converbs, i.e. non-finite adverbial verb forms. In Irano-Turkic varieties, most native subjunctors except some simple case marked converbs have been replaced by copies of prepositive free junctors. The resulting patterns are thus strongly frame-changing. See also Johanson (1999b).

7 Distributional Classes

Copied combinational patterns may lead to the emergence of new distributional classes, e.g. 'word classes'. On the model of Arabic-Persian and Russian adjective endings, some Turkic languages developed corresponding suffix classes using their own native devices. Combinational copying may lead to decreased or increased explicit marking. Omission of the possessive suffix in Germany Turkish (27a) instead of using a possessive suffix as in Standard Turkish (27b).

(27) a. Germany Turkish
‹Ben-im para var.›
I-GEN money existing
'I have money.' ⇐ German *Ich habe Geld.*

b. Standard Turkish
‹Ben-im para-m var.›
I-GEN money-POSS1SG existing
'I have money.'

Omission of possessive suffix occurs in cases such as (28). Compare (28a) with (28b).

(28) a. Germany Turkish
‹Diş-ler-i fırčala-dı.›
tooth-PL-ACC brush-PAST3SG
'X brushed the teeth.' ⇐ German *Er putzte die Zähne.*

b. Standard Turkish
⟨Diş-ler-in-i   fırça-la-dı.⟩
tooth-PL-POSS3SG-ACC brush-PAST3SG
'X brushed his/her teeth.'

Omission of the possessive suffix also occurs in possessive compound constructions. Turkish in Germany often exhibits cases such as *diš fïrča* 'tooth brush' instead of Standard Turkish ⟨diş fırça-sı⟩, with a final possessive suffix, taken over from the German compounding pattern in *Zahn-bürste*.

8 Degree of Complexity

Combinational copying can affect the degree of complexity, and lead to simplification, grammatical reduction, reduction of the formal inventory, e.g. in the complicated Turkish verb morphology. Underdifferentiation means a reduced use of devices, e.g. of the rich word order devices of Turkish. All these phenomena may also reflect independent erosion tendencies of the code in question.

9 Accommodation of Copies

All copies are accommodated to the Basic Code.

Phonic or phonological adaptation occurs in various cases. Accommodation of verbs is found in Turkish of Norway *å klatre yap-* 'to climb' ('to do climbing') taken over from Norwegian *å klatre* 'to climb', or Turkish of the Netherlands *kijken yap-* 'to look' taken over from Dutch *kijken* 'to look'. The intransitive German verb *jogg-en* and the Swedish verb *att jogg-a* 'to run at a jogtrot' are taken from the English verb *to jog* 'to push', 'to stir up', 'to shake'. In the Sweden Turkish expression *klättrade upp yap-tï* 'X climbed up' the past tense form of the Swedish verb *att klättra upp* 'to climb up' is combined with the Turkish verb *yap-* 'to do' (Bohnacker & Karakoç 2020).

German has taken over the English adjective *live* [laiv], meaning 'living', and represents it with the adjective *live*, though pronounced [lajf], with the aim to imitate the English pronunciation. Semantic properties of the original are replaced. No global copies will be totally identical in meaning to their originals, probably not even copies like these. The German adjective *live* means 'presented at the time it is happening, actually performed, not filmed or taped' taken over from English *live* 'being alive', 'being vivid', 'being fresh', 'flowing freely'. Turkish of Germany uses German *Heim* 'home' only in the meaning of 'hostel'. This restructuring of combinational properties may affect the combinability of the copies and also the internal organization of complex copies. The German adjective *live* [lajf] is also used as an adverb to imitate the English use.

Creative restructuring occurs in many cases. Turkish of Germany has thus *vaynak* 'Christmas' taken from *Weihnachten*, and *an yap-* 'to register' is used in the sense of [*sich*] *an-melden*. Swedish uses the noun *cykel* for 'bicycle', whereas English *cycle* in the sense of orbit, circulation, rotation has other equivalent words. The German word *Keks*, and the Swedish word *kex* 'biscuit', 'cookie' go back to the English plural *cakes*. Definite plural forms are German *die Keks-e* and Swedish *kex-en* 'the biscuits'.

CHAPTER 4

Code-Copying and Grammaticalization

The following considerations deal with code-copying and grammaticalization in the usual sense of a process by which typical lexical items lose some or all of their lexical meaning and become grammatical markers. Grammaticalization cannot be shared by codes as a result of code-copying. Shared grammaticalization in the sense of a parallel development of elements is however clearly possible. Compare the following contributions: Aikhenvald (2002, 2003), Aikhenvald & Dixon (2001), Corne (1995), Csató (2000), Heine & Kuteva (2003, 2005), Johanson (1974, 1994b, 1998c, 2005b, 2008a, 2011, 2013b, 2014b), Sapir (1921).

A copying procedure means that a copy of a Model Code element is inserted into a Basic Code according to some equivalence relation with a Target of Copying. Inserted copies are part of the Basic Code and immediately subject to its internal processes. The Target of Copying is analyzed and remodeled, often undergoing a development to a structurally more integrated element. The model element is copied at a specific stage of its code-internal development. The Target of Copying also has its own history and occupies a certain position in the Basic-Code internal development. Each instance of copying is a product of this coincidence. Copying cannot 'replicate' processes that have taken place in the Model Code. Diachronic developments are not copiable, even if they are known to the Basic Code speaker or to the linguist who analyzes the situation. Fresh copies, which often represent less advanced stages of grammaticalization than their models, may develop further, becoming increasingly similar to their models. Long-lasting intense contacts involving extensive copying processes may create convergent developments and highly isomorphic structures that make codes more compatible and intertranslatable. As a result of gradual isomorphic processes, typical of intense communication areas, so-called Sprachbunds, the codes may develop shared construction patterns and morphosyntactic markers (Johanson 2014a).

1 Isomorphism

As stated above, long-lasting intense contacts between one specific Basic Code and one specific Model Code—with high, perhaps increasing, degrees of bilingualism, at least among the Basic Code users—lead to increased isomorphism between the codes.

In cases of isomorphism, two or more languages share specific ways of creating grammatical markers. Such instances may be attributable to language contact, inheritance, i.e. common ancestorship, or universal principles of grammatical change. The relations between grammaticalization and grammatical copying raise intricate questions. See Aikhenvald (2001, 2002, 2003), Aikhenvald & Dixon (2001), and Heine & Kuteva (2003, 2005).

A process leading from lexemes to grammaticalized markers or from less grammatical to more grammatical functions is an operation by which content words lose some or all of their lexical properties and come to fulfill grammatical functions. Lexical items develop into function markers such as auxiliaries, case markers, inflections, and sentence relators. Examples from the Turkic speaking world are given in Johanson (2011).

Grammaticalization involves an input and an output, i.e. a Source of Grammaticalization, and a Target of Grammaticalization. Copying leading to grammatical function markers involve the following operations: Copies of free or bound markers of the Model Code are inserted into the frame of a Basic Code, into specific slots, 'insertion points', which are normally filled by their indigenous equivalents. This operation is based on the speaker's subjective assessment of the equivalence in a linguistic sense. The frame provided by the Basic Code accommodates the copies, which thus become part of the recipient system and may even replace their indigenous equivalents. There is thus, again, an input and an output, a Source of Copying and a Target of Copying.

2   Combined Scheme

The scheme of Grammaticalization combined with the scheme of Selective Grammatical Copying gives the following picture; see Figure 2.

Source of Grammaticalization   Source of Copying
⇓
Target of Grammaticalization   Target of Copying >   Copy

FIGURE 2   Selective grammatical copying

Basic Code users are confronted with a certain grammaticalized element of a Model Code. On the basis of some conceptual similarity, they establish, consciously or intuitively, an equivalence relation between this grammatical element and a suitable Target of Copying in their own code. They copy semantic and combinational properties of the Model Code item onto a matching Basic

Code item. The Basic Code item can now be used with a meaning and a combinability similar to that of the Model Code item.

Selective grammatical copying may create highly isomorphic structures that make codes more compatible and intertranslatable. To reduce the planning effort in forming sentences in the two codes, groups of advanced bilinguals often develop strategies that indicate common mental procedures for arranging the information (Matras 2006). Gradual isomorphic processes are typical of intense communication areas, in which codes develop shared constructional patterns and morphosyntactic markers regardless of genealogical boundaries. Even codes that differ strongly from each other in their vocabulary may become increasingly isomorphic.

Selective grammatical copying usually occurs when Basic Code users have reached a relatively advanced level of the Model Code. The copiability correlates with the stage of grammaticalization as reflected in different degrees of saliency of meaning and shape. Relatively salient items with more specific meanings and more elaborated shapes are more copiable than less salient items with more generalized meanings and reduced shapes.

Many types of selective grammatical copying serve isomorphism by creating convenient translation equivalents in the two interacting codes. This may mean combinational and/or semantic reorganization of grammatical devices in certain subsystems, e.g. in those of case markers and adpositions. Other types of selective grammatical copying entail a more radical restructuring of syntactic constructions on Model Code lines. These larger structures, e.g. constituent ordering patterns, tend to be copied in varieties of advanced bilinguals, i.e. when the two codes are already morphosyntactically similar and include copies of the less radical type.

3 Aikhenvald's 'Grammatical Accommodation' as a Case of Selective Copying

It is interesting to compare this with Aikhenvald's lucid concept of 'grammatical accommodation' (Aikhenvald 2002: 5, 239, cf. Adelaar 2004). As the following presentation of her analysis demonstrates, her approach is compatible with the Code-Copying Model and my account of increased isomorphism between codes in intensive contact through selective copying of grammatical features.

The fascinating features of multilingualism in Aikhenvald's study are based on obligatory exogamy and the sort of linguistic changes this entails in the Vaupés River Basin Linguistic area in the Amazonian area in Brazil, bordering on Colombia. It shows how languages belonging to two unrelated language families have come to resemble each other structurally, while avoiding any significant amount of lexical copying.

The East Tucanoan peoples of the Vaupés region practice a strict exogamy. They do not marry anyone speaking a native language identical to their own. There is extensive multilingualism: parents do not normally belong to the same language group. There is at least one non-Tucanoan group of Amazonian Indians that has adopted language-based rules of exogamy after it moved into the area, the Arawak-speaking Tariana. The marriage restrictions do not only affect speakers of the same language. The Tariana are not allowed to marry the Tucanoan Desano, considered to be their 'younger brothers'. A third group are speakers of the Maku languages, which cannot intermarry with the Tucanoans or with the Tariana because they are thought to be socially and culturally inferior. Therefore, language contact between speakers of Maku languages and the other language groups of the Vaupés is limited. The inhabitants of the Vaupés region were sensitive about language purity and highly valued language proficiency. Speakers avoided any kind of mixture. Natives who used words, morphemes, or even sounds associated with languages other than the one they were supposed to speak, are subject to scorn and ridicule. For Tariana this was a danger for its survival.

Through the policy of missionaries, which did not respect the marriage taboos of the natives, Tucano, one of the East Tucanoan languages, had become dominant in the area. For young Tariana people it was easier to express themselves in Tucano, rather than to being criticized for speaking poor Tariana. The insertion of East Tucanoan terms within Tariana speech, when the correct Tariana word is not at hand, is considered inappropriate. The Tariana are also enthusiastic in efforts to stimulate a continued use of the language.

The Tariana were originally organized as a hierarchically structured society with dialects corresponding to 'higher' and 'lower' social layers. The dialects constituted an internally differentiated continuum. Only two closely related dialects, Periquitos and Santa Rosa, associated with the lower strata of the society, remained viable. The attitudes towards innovation and copying are different. The Periquitos group is liberal in this respect, but also more successful in transmitting the language to the younger generation.

It is easy to appreciate the degree of change that has affected the Tariana language in its interaction with East Tucanoan. The language closely related to Tariana is Baniwa, with which some Tariana are familiar. Many differences separating Tariana and Baniwa are indicative of the transformation undergone by the former during the generations of contact by intermarriage with East Tucanoan speakers. Tariana has undergone an extensive asymmetrical influence from East Tucanoan.

Aikhenvald gives an overview of different types of contact phenomena and a discussion of general concepts, such as the notion of indirect diffusion, referring to cases where a language develops new categories copied from a contact language by using its own formal resources. Structural changes are classified as completed, ongoing, or discontinuous. Most changes achieved through indirect diffusion are completed, whereas direct diffusion usually involves ongoing changes. In Tariana, the contact situation has developed from an original state of multilateral diffusion, involving several varieties of East Tucanoan and Tariana, towards a more recent state of unilateral diffusion in which East Tucanoan Tucano is the dominant language. The Tariana use is an undesirable innovation by traditional speakers, even though their copied status is not always clearly established and alternatives may not be available. Indirect diffusion is most clearly visible in the morphology and morphosyntax. For Tariana, changes resulting from indirect diffusion do not necessarily mean simplification, because the language tends to accumulate native and foreign categories.

In contact phenomena involving the Tariana verb, an elaborated system has evolved in which tense and evidentiality categories are fused. Such systems occur in East Tucanoan languages, but not in the neighboring Arawak languages.

In Tariana, the evidentiality categories visual, nonvisual, inferred, and reported combine with the tenses present, recent past and remote past. The Tariana system has been extended by the introduction of a formal distinction between present and recent past in the reported category.

Tariana retains some of its most basic Arawak features. Some East Tucanoan clause types are being copied into Tariana, which seems to be more characteristic of younger speakers. Copula verbs are common in East Tucanoan, but not in Arawak, which may be a case of ongoing change. A general tendency towards isomorphism is found in the organization of discourse between East Tucanoan and Tariana.

The influence of Portuguese, a recent newcomer, is treated. The appearance of Portuguese lexical copies is received in a less negative way than East Tucanoan elements. One reason to avoid copying from Portuguese is that they may have already been incorporated in Tucano.

Language awareness is important, i.e. the question what sort of speech is considered 'correct' or 'incorrect' in the Tariana community. Aikhenvald's book conveys and analyzes the phenomena in a concrete and straightforward way and does not deal with superficial resemblances, as is often the case in studies of language contact.

4 Diachronic Processes Are Not Copiable

Let me summarize here what operational procedures make selective grammatical copying possible? Users of a Basic Code become aware of a certain grammatical element in a Model Code. On the basis of some conceptual similarity, an equivalence relation is established, consciously or intuitively, between the given Model Code element and a suitable Target of Copying in the Basic Code. The Target of Copying is a native lexical or grammatical element that seems to match the grammatical element of the Model Code and onto which the relevant properties of that element can be copied most naturally. The Target of Copying is reanalyzed and remodeled, e.g. assigned the relevant properties.

A simple example: Properties of a dual marker in a Model Code may be copied onto a numeral *two* as a Target of Copying to create a dual marker in a Basic Code.

Model Code: Source of Copying DUAL MARKER
⇓
Basic Code: Target of Copying *two* >   Copy: *two* DUAL MARKER
FIGURE 3   Copying dual markers

This example is not wholly imaginary. Thus, users of Tayo, a French-based creole in New Caledonia, seem to have copied properties of dual markers from the two Melanesian languages Drubéa and Cèmuhi onto the unit {-de} 'two' < French *deux* (Corne 1995).

There are certainly cases in which the chosen Target of Copying is similar to the Source of Grammaticalization of the model. For example, the dual marker of the Model Code may have developed from the numeral *two*, and the Basic Code users may have chosen its corresponding numeral as the Target of Copying. This establishes an analogous relation, but it does not mean that the Target of Copying has undergone or undergoes the grammaticalization process that has taken place in the Model Code. The copying act does not imply a repetition of this gradual process from less grammaticalized to more grammaticalized items. It is even irrelevant whether the choice of the target is motivated or not by knowledge of the diachronic Source of Grammaticalization of the model, i.e. whether the Basic Code users are guided or not by the etymological relation between the model and its Source of Grammaticalization.

Heine & Kuteva (2003, 2005) contend that contact-induced grammatical change is essentially subject to the same principles of grammaticalization as changes that are not induced by contact. They suppose that speakers can "replicate a grammaticalization process they assume to have taken place in language M", which is the Model Code (2005: 92). This process is not shared by the Model Code and the Basic Code as a result of copying. Basic Code users cannot cope with diachronic processes that have already taken place.

The element is copied at a certain stage of its code-internal development along a specific grammaticalization path. The Target of Copying has its own history and occupies a certain position in the internal development of the Basic Code. Each instance of copying is a product of this coincidence. The elements involved are the *result* of processes that have been reached prior to the moment of coincidence. The copying act immediately turns the Target of Copying into a grammatical marker similar to that of the Source of Copying. What is coped is the *result* of a grammaticalization process, not the process itself. Diachronic processes are never copiable, even if they happen to be recoverable by the speakers themselves or by linguists. If the copying act could capture a grammaticalization process, it would be a backward move, a violation of the unidirectionality principle assumed for grammaticalization rules.

5   Lexical and Grammatical Targets of Copying

The Target of Copying may be a lexical element of the Basic Code that seems to match the Model Code item onto which its properties can be copied most naturally. This Model Code item is reanalyzed and remodeled, i.e. assigned the relevant properties.

A grammaticalization process in a Model Code may have the lexical element meaning 'two' as input and a grammatical dual marker as output. Basic Code users establish an analogy with the lexical element for 'two' in their own code and copy properties of the Model Code dual marker onto it as a Target of Copying.

The Target of Copying may also be an indigenous grammatical element of the Basic Code. In the Turkic language Karaim, syntactic properties of the Slavic case marker with instrumental and comitative function, 'by means of' and 'together with' are copied onto the suffixed postposition {-bA} 'with', e.g. (29).

(29) Copying the function of case marking in Northwest Karaim
    Ol   vaxt-ta   ata-m   ed'i   ür'ät'üv'č'ü-b'ä.
    that time-LOC father-POSS1SG COP-PAST3SG teacher-POSTP.with
    'At that time my father was a teacher.'

In (29), the predicate 'teacher' is marked with the Karaim postposition 'with'. Thus, the Karaim postposition has acquired the syntactic distribution of the Russian case marker with the result that in certain syntactic constructions its use is obligatory (Csató 2000: 274).

6 Awareness of Sources

Grammaticalization processes are long and complex, often extending over centuries. The Basic Code speakers are mostly not aware of the processes. In certain cases, the relation may be clearer because the lexical source is still detectable or even synchronically present in the Model Code. Basic Code speakers with a good knowledge of the Model Code may then be able to equate it with a lexical element in their own code. They may, for example, choose their numeral for 'two' as the Target of Copying in order to create a dual marker. This establishes an analogous relation, an isomorphic relationship. But even if Basic Code speakers are aware of the completed grammaticalization process, this is irrelevant for their act of copying. The only thing copied is the output of the process. The only thing shared by the items of the two codes is similarity in meaning and combinability. The copying act captures a synchronic cut in the developments of the two items. The target of copying has not undergone any process by which it has become increasingly grammatical. It is immediately used as a grammatical marker without such a process. Grammaticalization is mostly a long way to create grammatical markers. Copying is a kind of shortcut, an operation leading directly to the goal.

The impression that the copy relates to the Source of Copying in the same way as the Source of Copying relates to the Source of Grammaticalization is illusory. The grammatical marker is created in analogy with the relation between the Target of Grammaticalization and its Source. It is an *analogical* creation. The Source of Copying is nothing more than a *simulated* Source of Grammaticalization. The relation helps the Basic Code speakers to find a matching Target of Copying. But the copying act does not repeat the gradual process from less grammaticalized to more grammaticalized stages. The analogy concerns grammatical markers which are similar in function, possibly also in material shape, but which differ in origin.

7 Use after Copying

Contact-induced copying thus does not lead to shared input and output of grammaticalization. There is, however, also a life after copying. Fresh copies often represent less advanced stages of grammaticalization than their models with respect to semantic, combinational and frequential properties.

The semantic functions of copies have often not reached the stage of the originals. They have not undergone the stages of grammaticalization that their models have gone through. Their use is frequently pragmatically determined. They often have lower text frequencies than their originals. Their use is often optional rather than obligatory. They often have a lower degree of combinability, being less generally applicable to contexts. It might sometimes even be difficult to decide whether fresh copies already represent fully grammaticalized categories.

For example, the use of newly copied aspectual-temporal elements is often contextually restricted and optional. This is also true of Sorbian, Czech, and Slovenian definite articles copied from Germanic, or the Basque indefinite article copied from Romance. Heine and Kuteva note: "wherever there is sufficient evidence, it turns out that the replica construction is less grammaticalized than the corresponding model construction" (2005: 101).

If we would take the copying act itself to imply a grammaticalization process, these phenomena would have to be viewed as backward movements, cases of reversed directionality, violations of the unidirectionality principle assumed for grammaticalization paths.

Once copied, the items may continue developing their grammatical functions. This is a matter of internal developments in the Basic Code. The development is code-internal and gradual. In their further development, the copies may undergo grammaticalization processes of their own acquiring features typical of more advanced stages, becoming increasingly similar to their models. As Heine and Kuteva remark: "contact-induced language change is a complex process and not infrequently extends over centuries, or even millennia" (2005: 5).

It is rather the code-internal, gradual processes subsequent to the copying acts that are complex and long-running. The copies may develop more general grammatical meanings, be used in wider ranges of contexts, get an increased degree of obligatoriness, and undergo erosion in the sense of phonetic substance. This makes it increasingly difficult to decide which of two similar grammatical elements, which have emerged in chronologically remote contact situations, was originally the model and which one was the copy.

8   'Inherited Grammaticalization'

The output of a grammaticalization process in an ancestral code may be defined and developed further by its daughter codes. So-called 'inherited grammaticalization' can only mean inherited and developed *results* of grammaticalization. The daughters do not inherit or repeat any process. But they may reflect processes that once took place in the ancestral code and represent them analogically. It is a given element of the ancestral code that had both a lexical and a grammatical function. This ambiguity may be mirrored in the daughter codes. The emergence of Romance future markers is a well-known case of inheritance. French, Italian, Spanish, and Portuguese possess lexical verbs meaning 'to leave', e.g. Italian *avere*, all going back to Latin *habere*. This verb was the Source of Grammaticalization for the creation of future markers in Vulgar Latin, i.e. *cantari habet* 'has to be sung'. The daughters inherited the outcome of a completed grammaticalization process, but they certainly did not share this process.

Developments of this kind may result from parallel linguistic drift in the sense of Sapir (1921: 171–172). Sapir observed that languages that have long been disconnected often "pass through the same or strikingly similar phases". A number of genealogically related languages may display a specific type of grammaticalization, which is too late to belong to the common ancestry and cannot be explained by copying. The reason for its appearance might be a tendency that occurs independently in each of the languages, but along parallel lines of development. The codes in question may have undergone certain structurally formed changes, cases of analogical grammaticalization. But it remains inexplicable how the same grammaticalization processes would have occurred repeatedly and independently in the individual daughter codes.

Time erases most traces of grammaticalization and copying processes. But it might sometimes still be possible to decide whether the isomorphic creation of grammatical markers is a result of remote linguistic relationship, contact, or universal metaphoric tendencies.

Robbeets (2012) mentions parallel creation of grammatical markers in the Transeurasian languages and the possible genealogical relation between these languages. The argumentation includes examples of relatively rare processes that may have been completed or that are on their way towards completion in a hypothetical ancestral language. Languages displacing functional equivalent and phonetically similar bound grammatical markers may have inherited results of the old grammaticalization process. If the ancestral language possessed co-occurring input and output forms of the relevant grammaticalization processes, the situation may be preserved as a variation in the descendant languages.

If the linguistic mother used the word 'one' as an indefinite article, this duality is neither the outcome of contact-induced interdialect copying, nor a case of shared or inherited grammaticalization. It is rather the inherited result of a grammaticalization process in the ancestral language. The complete result has been preserved as an isomorphic relation. The indefinite use does not occur in the Turkic languages Chuvash and Yakut, maybe due to non-Turkic contact influences. It might also be a case of inherited variation in two languages that left the common area of grammaticalization before the process had been brought to completion.

Functionally equivalent and phonetically similar bound grammatical markers witnessing of inherited result of rare grammaticalization processes are strong arguments for genealogical relatedness. A candidate would be the Transeurasian pattern involving markers that may be interpreted as causatives or passive formatives: 'to let do' or 'to be done', signaling that the range of the action transcends the domain of the first actant, which is then interpreted as source, 'initiator' of the goal, and 'patient' of the action (Johanson 1974, 1998a: 55–56). This pattern may have existed in a possible Transeurasian protolanguage. But it is also found outside the Transeurasian group, e.g in Caucasian languages.

9 Conceivable Carry-over-Copying of Evidentials

Turkic evidentials have proved to be attractive for copying into non-Turkic languages. Turkic evidentials indicate that the narrated event is stated by reference to its reception by a conscious recipient. The source is not specified; it can be inference, hearsay or perception (Johanson 2021: 651). There are two types of Turkic evidentials:

(i) Postterminal verb forms which are formally identical to verbal nominals, built with accentable suffixes, e.g. {-mIš} or {-GAn}, which can attach directly to verb stems.
(ii) Unaccentable enclitic temporally indifferent copula particles of the type *i-miš* and *e-kän*, which can attach to nominal or verbal nominal stems.

Eastern South Slavic languages possess special reportive, narrative, or non-testimonial forms, evidential categories signaling that a given utterance is based on indirect evidence. The opposition of the South Slavic participles *xodel*, derived from the imperfect stem, and *xodil*, derived from the aorist stem, parallels the distinction between the verb forms *bar-a-yan* (intraterminal) 'going' and *bar-yan* (postterminal) 'having gone' in some Kipchak Turkic languages of the Pontic area (Johanson 1996a). The Kipchak form *bar-yan e-*

kän, a combination with the enclitic evidential copula *e-kän*, expresses the evidential meaning 'has/had reportedly gone'.

Bulgarian has a corresponding copular item with isomorphic functional and combinational properties. This temporally indifferent Bulgarian particle *bil* functions as an evidential marker which in the combinations such as *bil xodil* just like the corresponding Kipchak form means 'has/had reportedly gone'. This correspondence can be explained as a selective and combinational copy of the function of the Kipchak evidential copula on a native Bulgarian element, a carry-over process which might have taken place in an originally Turkic-speaking population that shifted to South Slavic (Johanson 1996a, 1998c). On the related Persian evidential categories see Windfuhr (1982).

CHAPTER 5

Remodeling Languages

This chapter will summarize some features of remodeling languages with respect to copying, conventionalization, and grammaticalization.

1 Code-Internal Development

Copying is a punctual interaction across code borders. The further development of copies is code-internal and gradual. Once a copy is conventionalized, it is subject to the internal processes of the Basic Code. It may be dealt with in the same way as non-copied innovations. Selective grammatical copies may be further grammaticalized, acquiring features typical of advanced stages, developing more general grammatical meanings, being used in wider ranges of contexts, increasing their use and degree of obligatoriness, being decategorialized into clitics and affixes, eroded in the sense of loss of phonetic substance. All this is solely a matter of code-internal development. Copies representing advanced stages of grammaticalization have few chances to develop further, except for taking on highly general functions and being subject to material erosion.

In their further developments, copies often become indistinguishable from native elements. They may survive and develop further, even after their models have vanished. A copy may also become more and more similar to its model, which makes it increasingly difficult to tell which of two similar grammatical elements in chronologically remote contact situations was the model and which one was the copy.

2 Remodeling the Basic-Code Frame

With increasingly more conventionalized grammatical copies, the Basic Code frame may change considerably.

Changes of the Basic Code frame, into which copies are inserted, are produced by global copies of grammatical markers, selective copies of grammatical markers, and selective copies of combinational patterns. Successive copying processes of different kinds promote each other, and may lead to snowball effects with respect to the remodeling of the Basic Code frame; see further on.

Copying of constructional patterns goes hand in hand with progressive selective copying of grammatical markers. Older copies prepare the ground for new copies. At each stage of development, the Basic Code frame must be described anew. Every given new norm is deviated from by new 'marked' copying. All new systems offer frames for further *inšā* and conventionalization. On frame-changing developments, see in particular Johanson (1999a).

Combinational copying creates new equivalence positions for further copying of grammatical markers. On the other hand, copied markers trigger copying of combinational properties, e.g. of new constructional patterns in which the markers are contained. The use of a copied grammatical marker may be tied to a certain position in a pattern. For example, Tariana of northwestern Brazil has copied Portuguese subordination markers, which has triggered the copying of a Portuguese combinational pattern, according to which a complement clause follows the main clause predicate instead of preceding it (Aikhenvald 2002: 182).

In high-copying codes, complex and combined processes may essentially reshape the morphosyntactic frame, adding new typological features to it. The codes can acquire seemingly disparate features. It is even "perfectly possible for a language to copy structures that might appear to be 'typologically inconsistent' with the rest of its structure" (Comrie 2002: xi). A precondition for this is that the new features are not imported or transferred foreign elements, but just copies adapted to Basic Code structures.

Gradual processes extending over centuries may involve multiple layers and complex combinations of copying, conventionalization and subsequent code-internal grammaticalization. Established copies which are considered part of the 'inherited' inventory may be the final result of long series of changes, and they cannot easily be traced back to the copying act.

3   Convergence and Divergence

There may be convergent developments between the codes, irrespective of their genealogical affiliations. Increasing structural adoption, however, reduces the degree of isomorphism. Convergence implies reciprocity in the sense that codes, as a result, become more similar to each other. The driving force may be different. If the convergence is due to bilateral influence, two codes move toward each other, acquiring more and more common characteristics. The convergence is, however, mostly due to unilateral influence, a one-sided inclination, with one code approaching the other and becoming more similar to it (Johanson 2005a: 4; cf. Clyne 2003: 79).

The opposite is divergence. Two codes may bilaterally draw apart from a common norm, acquiring dissimilar properties. For example, codes descended from a common ancestor evolve into different forms when used under different conditions. The divergence may, however, also be caused by unilateral influence, with one of the codes deviating one-sidedly, turning aside, and branching off from a common norm.

Extensive copying processes may lead codes to converge strongly with others, including unrelated ones, and also to diverge strongly from their genealogical heritage. On the other hand, codes do not abandon their heritage and fuse with unrelated contact codes. No high-copying code seems to have turned into the Model Code it has copied extensively from (Johanson 2002b).

4   Converging through Selective Copying

English has influenced European languages in various ways. A crucial difference is whether English words are globally copied or translated, i.e. their meaning selectively copied on native items. For instance, English has computer related verbs of the type *to down-load* and *to up-load*. Spanish has *des-cargar* 'to download', Hungarian *le-tölt*, i.e. 'down' + 'to load', and Chinese has 下載 *xiàzài* 'download', Swedish *ned-ladda* or *ner-ladda*, e.g. *Jag vill ladda ner artikeln* 'I want to download the article'. In German, the global copy with German morphology *downloaden* can be used, e.g. *Ich möchte den Artikel downloaden*. These expressions demonstrate a convergence in the lexicon although most of these expressions are not global copies of English words.

A very important feature in some European languages is German syntactic influence. Swedish and Hungarian syntax have taken over strong German influence. It is highly interesting to compare the results in the related languages. There is a very similar Swedish influence on Finnish syntax.

The Swedish item *före* is a preposition that takes nominal complements, e.g. *före sommaren* 'before the holiday'. *Innan* is a conjunction that introduces adverbial clauses, e.g. *innan du kommer* 'before you come'. However, *innan* is now also used as a preposition, e.g. *innan sommaren* 'before the summer', *innan kvällen* 'before the evening' and even *innan dess* 'before that', with the old genitive pronominal form *dess* 'its'. Note that English *before* can be used in both combinations. This combinational property has been copied on the Swedish items *före* and *innan*. Both are used in spoken colloquial style as a preposition and as a conjunction. The distinction between prepositional and conjunctional use is maintained in other cases. For instance, *till* is a preposition, e.g. *till kvällen* 'until the evening'. The conjunction *tills* introduces adverbial clauses, e.g. *Vi väntar tills/till dess att han kommer* 'We wait until he arrives'. The preposition *till* cannot be used as a conjunction, e.g. **till han kommer*.

Another Swedish example is the anglicism *Han är större än mej* ⟨he is big-COMP than me⟩ influenced by English 'He is bigger than me'. In a similar way, under the influence of English *Han drack det alldeles själv* ⟨he drink.PAST it quite self⟩ 'He drank it quite alone' is often used instead of the correct Swedish *Han drack det alldeles ensam* ⟨he drank it quite alone⟩. The word *själv* 'self' is used instead of *ensam* 'alone'. There is a big difference between drinking by yourself, without help, and drinking alone, that is without company.

5   Momentary, Habitualized, and Conventionalized Copies

Insertional copying acts may be momentary, ephemeral phenomena, corresponding to Weinreich's 'nonce-borrowing' (1953: 11). They begin in individuals, more precisely in the *mind* of individuals, which may also mean intuitive and unconscious copying. Copying grammatical function units and patterns is certainly less conscious than copying content units, which speakers and also linguists tend to be more aware of. On the other hand, individual speakers who perform an originary act of copying, normally have some degree of knowledge of the Model Code. Selective grammatical copying presupposes some degree of familiarity with Model Code structures and some ability to analyze them.

- Code copies may habitualize, i.e. become used habitually, and thus have more lasting effects, with various degrees of recurrence in the individual.
- Code copies may also become more or less conventionalized, i.e. have effects on the linguistic behavior of speech communities of varying sizes.
- Code copying starting as momentary performance phenomena may thus have diachronic effects. The path leading to conventionalizing is a continuum of changes in the sociolinguistic status, of degrees of recurrence in the speech community.

So-called 'integration', which leads from structurally less integrated to more integrated copies, is a different development, and not an unequivocal or necessary criterion for distinguishing degrees of conventionalization.

When a copy is conventionalized, the degree of Model Code knowledge of the individual speakers is irrelevant. Deviations originally perceived as 'interference' may establish themselves as new sets of norms, even replacing their Basic Code equivalents. The processes lead to linguistic change. New systems are created in which conventionalized copies form integral parts. They are now facts of linguistic history and thus objects of historical linguistics. There may also be further diffusion, the code-copying variety becoming the unmarked way of speaking in ever-expanding groups. Copies may, however, also be unsuccessful or only reach a very limited diffusion. And they can, of course, also be subject to deconventionalization and loss.

CHAPTER 6

Turkic Family-External Contacts

Examples from the development of Turkic languages are especially telling with respect to the questions discussed here. The reason is that they have been in contact with a high number of other languages and gone through various situations with them.

Local Turkicized groups have sometimes been formed without major demographic changes. A case in point is the introduction of Azeri in Transcaucasia and Iran by relatively small Seljuk groups, which led to gradual supplanting of several existing regional and local Iranian, and Caucasian codes.

Similar scenarios are probable in many other areas, i.e. cases in which the advanced political organization of incoming groups have led to linguistic dominance. The copiability of lexical items, derivational morphology, inflectional morphology, syntactic patterns, and phonological elements varies a good deal. It is not always easy to distinguish effects of take-over and carry-over copying. Carry-over copying of phonological elements is, however, mostly relatively easy to recognize. Among the numerous non-Turkic contact varieties, some are Indo-European, e.g. Iranian, Slavic, Greek, Armenian, and modern West European. The non-Indo-European varieties include Mongolic, Uralic, Tungusic, Yeniseic, Chinese, Caucasian, and Arabic. Speakers of Turkic have taken over copies of foreign elements in their varieties. Speakers of non-Turkic languages have carried over indigenous elements into their varieties of Turkic. The contacts have mostly taken place in specific influence spheres. Areas of intensive contact have been Central Asia, Anatolia, the Balkans, Transcaucasia, the Volga-Ural region, South Siberia, and recently also Northwestern Europe. Turkic varieties have participated in various Sprachbunds, linguistic convergence areas. Early contacts in Siberia of Oghur ancestral groups with speakers of Samoyedic and Mongolic are attested by mutual lexical copies (Róna-Tas 1980, 1988, 1991).

Contacts with Iranian have been of paramount importance. Speakers of East Old Turkic were in early contact with Soghdian, even if this did not lead to widespread bilingualism. The old language Karakhanid was strongly influenced by Soghdian and Persian. The contacts with Iranian continued to affect East Middle Turkic and its successors. Persian has exerted a deep influence on other languages and dialects of Iran and is clearly observable in syntax, morphology, and phonology. Some Turkic languages have come under Persian influence relatively late, e.g. Noghay in the 17th–18th centuries. The Arabic-Persian impact on Turkic languages of the Islamic cultural sphere has been extraordinarily intense. Languages such as Ottoman, Chaghatay, Uzbek, Uyghur, Tatar, Azeri, Turkmen, Kazakh, and Kirghiz, display innumerable take-over elements of Arabic-Persian origin. Elements of Arabic origin are normally not the result of direct exposure to Arabic. They have usually been copied from Persian.

Many elements of Mongolic origin are found in languages of the Mongolic sphere of influence, e.g. in Old Uyghur of the Yüan period and in modern languages such as Tatar, Kazakh, Kirghiz, Sayan Turkic, and Yakut. Mongolic varieties have taken over numerous copies from Turkic.

In the Russian-dominated area, Russian has achieved dominance as the common language of administration, education, and media. Smaller languages were exposed to the enormous influence from Russian and had low chances of survival. Languages of the Russian sphere of influence have undergone a more or less strong Russian impact in lexicon, phonology, and syntax. It is strongest in languages that had early contacts with Russian, e.g. Chuvash, Tatar, Kazakh, and Yakut. The modern languages Karaim and Gagauz have been subject to excessive copying from Slavic in phonology, syntax, and lexicon (Csató 2000, 2006).

Greek influence has been especially considerable. Greek substrata are present in several Turkic varieties, including Southwest Karaim, Urum, and the Turkish Black Sea dialects of Trabzon and Rize. Southwest Karaim displays phonological peculiarities that are not, however, found in Northwest Karaim. This is probably the result of Greek influence prior to the time of emigration from Crimea to Galicia. A fascinating code is Turkish as spoken in Western Thrace, which borders on Eastern Macedonia in the west, Bulgaria in the north, Turkey in the east, and the Aegean Sea in the south. It is an important issue how the variety has been influenced by the contact sources, namely the Greek and Turkish standard acrolects, varieties of speech that are considered most suitable for formal occasions, and basilects that are considered suitable for informal contexts by speakers. This is a most valuable approach to tell apart lower and higher contact sources.

Questions of possible prehistorical code-copying are central in controversies concerning Pre-Turkic or Proto-Turkic. Opponents of an Altaic or a Transeurasian kinship hypotheses assume different layers of areal copies between the families involved. Lexical elements common to Turkic and Mongolic are explained as Mongolic copies from a Turkic dialect more or less close to Proto-Turkic. Elements common to Turkic, Mongolic, and Tungusic are considered to have been copied into Tungusic from Mongolic. Speakers of predecessors of Tungusic languages such as Evenki and Even are assumed to have copied Mongolic words during their westward migrations. It is assumed that Turkic later continued to influence Mongolic, whereas Mongolic continued to influence Tungusic. Discussions of these glottogenetic issues must reckon with the fluctuating and polyglot character of the old tribal confederacies, complex areal interactions owing to permanent displacements, divergence, and convergence tendencies, as well as shared substrata.

Grammatical suffixes that stand closest to the primary stem in the agglutinative structure, namely those of actionality and diathesis, are less copiable. Peripheral morphemes are the most copiable morphemes (Johanson 1992, 2002c, 2008b). Personal clitics are the most peripheral elements in verbal inflection. It is important for genealogical questions whether they are stable features, relatively resistant to copying, apt to serve as criteria for genealogical classifications. They are in fact relatively instable, easily copiable and often subject to analogical changes. On the contact history of Turkic see Comrie (1995, 2002). The attractiveness of Turkic for copying is dealt with in Johanson (1992b, 2002c).

Speakers of East Old Turkic once migrated from South Siberia to Eastern Turkestan, present-day Xinjiang. The incoming speakers of East Old Turkic encountered resident groups of speakers of Iranian languages such as Tokharian and Soghdian. These eventually acquired the incoming elements as a second language code, and carried over phonological first language features to it.

The Turkic lexicon, which was widely known in the region, was copied in large part along with phonological features. The carried-over features were preserved as a substratum when the Iranian groups shifted to Turkic. Uyghur was thus subject to carry-over copying from Indo-European. Populations carried over phonetic features to their brand of Turkic. Large non-Turkic groups shifted to Turkic. After non-Turkic shifts to Turkic, these features were preserved as a substratum. Uyghur displays many features that are lacking or are uncommon in other Turkic languages. Certain vowel changes and other phonological irregularities can be interpreted as Indo-European substratum phenomena. For instance umlaut in Uyghur such as *belik* 'fish' < *balïk. Modern Uyghur shows traces of bidirectional copying: both take-over and carry-over.

The case of Uzbek, which was influenced by Persian, is comparable. Speakers of East Old Turkic, including the Karakhanid variety, migrated to Transoxiana, the land between the Oxus and Amudarya rivers, where they took over numerous elements from the Iranian codes spoken by large resident populations. The resident Iranian-speaking population eventually acquired the incoming Turkic code as a second language code, carrying over phonological first language features to it.

After they had shifted to Turkic, the features were preserved as a substratum. The result is a Persian-influenced vowel system. The vowel inventory underwent centralizations that affected the phonemic distinctions /ä/ vs. /a/, /ö/ vs. /o/, /ü/ vs. /u/, and /i/ vs. /ï/. The phoneme /å/, which corresponds to /a/ in most Turkic languages, is realized as a slightly labialized back vowel [ɒ]. Considerable syntactic features were also carried over to this brand of Turkic. In the case of Uzbek and Azeri, large non-Turkic populations carried over both phonetic and syntactic features to their brand of Turkic, and this brand became predominant.

A small number of Seljuk speakers of an Oghuz Turkic that was influenced by the unrelated language Persian migrated into the Transcaucasian area. Although Turkic was introduced by a small elite group, it gradually supplanted a number of regional languages. Numerous resident speakers of Iranian and Caucasian languages acquired this incoming code as a second language variety and carried over some phonological first language features to it. After the shift to Turkic, some of their primary-code features were preserved as a substratum. Azeri was mildly influenced by Persian, which had already been influenced and simplified by Turkic.

Speakers of Oghur Turkic migrated into the Volga-Kama area around the end of the 8th century. Resident speakers of Finnic languages, e.g. Mari, acquired it as a second language code and carried over phonological features from their first language to their own brand of it. The resulting phonology in Chuvash was confusing because the languages were genealogically unrelated. Chuvash displays numerous irregular and complicated sound changes, especially among the vowels, whose correspondences with Common Turkic vowels are amazingly unsystematic. The development of Chuvash was complicated by a series of sound changes and replacements; however, it remained typologically similar to other Turkic languages in syntax and lexicon. After the Finnic groups had shifted to Turkic, phonological features of their varieties were preserved as a substratum. The influence was so strong that Chuvash was incorrectly considered a Finno-Ugric language by earlier scholars. The language is, however, clearly Turkic in lexicon and grammar (Johanson 2000a). It was just subject to phonological carry-over copying from Finnic Model Codes. Chuvash is an example of profound phonological carry-over copying.

The speakers of the ancestor of Yakut once migrated northward from South Siberia. They first took over lexical and other elements from Mongolic on the shore of Lake Baikal. Advancing further north, they encountered resident speakers of Tungusic, who acquired the Turkic language as a second language code, carrying over to it syntactic, morphological, and phonological features from their first language. When the Tungusic groups shifted to Turkic, the features of their own language were preserved as a substratum. Yakut did not undergo carry-over copying of Tungusic phonology of the sort that caused confusion in Chuvash. Tungusic lexical copies are rare in Turkic. Few Tungusic lexemes were carried over to standard Yakut, as is typical of a substratum situation. Standard Yakut does have a few lexical copies belonging to the domains of husbandry and everyday life, e.g. *jiä* 'house'. Non-standard Yakut dialects have some hundred words copied from Tungusic. Dolgan, a north Siberian relative, displays numerous Evenki lexical copies. Yakut has not copied any derivational suffixes from Tungusic, but the derivational system is strongly influenced by take-over copying from Mongolic.

Local non-Turkic codes have been abandoned in favor of intrusive immigrant Turkic codes. But they have caused substrata of carry-over copying.

Carry-over of lexical elements has been limited, but there are changes in grammatical structures. Even inflectional morphemes have been carried over in a few cases. The major effects of carry-over copying are found in the phonology, i.e. sound changes due to inherited articulation habits.

Codes of Turkicized groups represent the results of efforts to pronounce Turkic sounds. Though nearly all Turkic languages show systematic sound correspondences within their genealogical family, carry-over copying has led to irregularities in some cases. Minority groups rarely copy over lexicon. This would not be understood by the majority. If the Model Codes are unrelated to Turkic codes, phonology becomes discrepant. Umlaut is certainly not an attractive feature to take over. But it can be carried over (Uyghur). Minority groups shifting to Turkic have displayed their own characteristic pronunciation habits. On the pronunciation of Turkish by minorities in Turkey, see Kowalski (1934: 993).

Non-substratic Turkic languages mainly display results of take-over influence. Kazakh represents a normal Turkic type, without recognizable substrata. But it has lexical copies from Mongolic and other languages.

The degree of bilingualism and plurilingualism in older speaker communities is impossible to judge on. Multiple model languages may have resulted in homogeneity. Codes may be subject to limited or extensive copying, determined by social circumstances and attitudes. Differences can be observed in extent and degree of copying. Turkic communities have always been ready to mix socially with other groups. Nomadic groups have had a great freedom to modify their codes.

Take-over copying is an intense form of contact. Languages that were more stable were weakly affected. Those that were less stable were strongly affected.

Take-over copying typically occurs in asymmetrical contact situations when speakers of a dominated language take over copies from a dominant language.

Selectional copies of phonetic and phonological features, have had an impact on the original phonological system. An example is palatalization of consonants in Turkic dominated by Slavic languages. The underlying Turkic principle of sound harmony is maintained, but the realization of the sounds is accommodated to Slavic phonology.

Frequential copying has resulted in more frequent use of variants that correspond to structures found in the second language. For example, the possessive construction of the locative type *M'än'-d'ä bart uŋ-lu yüv* ⟨I-LOC existent big house⟩ cf. Russian *У меня большой дом* ⟨by I-GEN big house⟩ 'I have a big house' has become relatively frequent in Karaim at the expense of the typically more frequent genitive structure.

CHAPTER 7

Code-Copying in Some Large Languages of the World

The rules of code-copying have so far been presented in a systematic way. Now some further examples of the strength of languages in their roles of take-over and carry-over copying will be given in a more diverse and a less methodical way. The mostly trivial existence of copying processes in the past and their contributions to far-reaching comprehensive communication systems will be illustrated. Let us first look briefly at some selected important languages of the world, English, Chinese, Arabic, and Russian. Some examples of copying processes will help to gain an impression of the linguistic effects of various types of copying which have taken place in these languages and contributed to their present shape.

1   English

The first language is English, an incredibly powerful system. Its modern position is, of course, fundamentally different from its role at older stages of its development. It is thus known that Old English took once over plenty of global and selective copies from the then dominating Old Norse language. "The best-researched cluster of examples is the borrowing of the Norse-derived plural forms *they* and *them* of the personal pronoun and the conjunction *though*" (Lutz 2012: 31). The take-over copying of these function words was surely facilitated by the genealogical closeness of the two languages. The high number of Romance lexical copies in English is assigned to the dominating role of Old French at the period of copying (Lutz 2012: 15).

English is known to have taken over copies from other languages in all conceivable contact situations. In our days, English, as a highly successful language of international communication, opens the door for carry-over copying in many linguistic communities. Non-first speakers of English in areas dominated by English are taking over features from English and carrying over materials from their own languages to the different forms of English that they use. English has, as we know, over time split into 'English-World-Wide', i.e. various 'Englishes' in the world.

A well-known example is Indian English. In India, English has been a dominating, highly prestigious language spoken in multilingual settings. Several

© LARS JOHANSON, 2023 | DOI:10.1163/9789004548459_007

varieties of Indian English are used as second language in India. For a listener the most conspicuous features are some phonological elements carried over as a result of selective material copying from native Indian vernaculars. Gargesh (2008) enlists the most important features including the retroflex pronunciation of t and d, e.g. *certificate* [sərʈifikeːʈ] and *London* [ləndən] and in some varieties the absence of the dental fricatives θ and δ. The aspirated voiceless stop t is pronounced for θ, as in thought [tɔt] and d for δ as in *then* [den] (Gangesh 2008: 237–238).

2 Chinese

Chinese belongs to the Sinitic branch of the Sino-Tibetan group of languages, which also includes Tibeto-Burman. The Sino-Tibetan group constitutes the world's second largest language family after Indo-European. It is spoken by the ethnic Han Chinese majority and a multitude of minorities. Standard Chinese, known in China as Putonghua, is based on the Mandarin dialect of Beijing. This variety is the official national language for the Chinese mainland.

It is obvious that Chinese must be defined as a language group and not a language. Its spoken varieties are considered by native speakers to be variants of a single language. They are, however, classified by linguists as separate languages within a family that includes rather divergent varieties. Most classifications of Chinese varieties posit regional groups based on phonetic developments starting from the period of Middle Chinese.

The Swedish linguist Bernhard Karlgren (1889–1978), who had trained his capability to describe linguistic varieties in his homeland, produced a rewarding addition to the knowledge of Chinese varieties in this sense (Malmqvist 1979). He carried out the first systematic survey of modern varieties of Chinese. He therefore used the oldest known rime tables as descriptions of the sounds of the rime dictionaries. He believed that the resulting categories reflected the speech standard of the capital Chang'an of the Sui (581–618) and Tang (618–690, 705–907) dynasties. He interpreted the many distinctions as narrow transcriptions of the precise sounds of the language. Karlgren's transcription involved a large number of consonants and vowels. His notation is still widely used, its symbols being based on Johan August Lundell's Swedish Dialect Alphabet, the so-called 'Landsmålsalfabetet'. All reconstructions of Middle Chinese since Karlgren have followed his approach, which has, however, also been criticized.

The Chinese varieties are typically classified into several groups, e.g. Mandarin, Wu, Min, Xiang, Gan, Hakka, and Yue. They are mostly claimed to be unintelligible to each other. All varieties of Chinese are tonal, at least to some degree. Standard Chinese is based on the Beijing dialect of Mandarin. It was adopted in the 1930s and is now an official language of the People's Republic of China and the Republic of China (Taiwan). It is also one of the four official languages of Singapore, of which the other languages are English, Malay, and Tamil. The written form of Chinese, which is shared by all literate users, employs logograms.

Chinese has an extremely high prestige in China and has been claimed not to have been influenced by other languages. Knowledge of it is the absolute condition for advancement and missing knowledge is actually not welcome. Chinese exerts strong influence on the other languages in its environment. On the other hand, it has also taken over certain lexemes from these languages. Because non-Chinese speakers everywhere carry-over features of their own languages when speaking Chinese, their local varieties of Chinese are characterized by carried-over non-Chinese features. For instance, Uyghur-Chinese bilingualism in Xinjiang has deeply influenced the local variety of Mandarin, which exhibit global lexical copies of Uyghur items, e.g. *piqiake* 'knife' ⇐ Uyghur *pičak*, and also selectively copied features from Uyghur. For example, the combinational properties of the general Uyghur plural have been copied on the Chinese plural marker *men*, which in standard Mandarin attaches only to nouns denoting an indefinite number of people. Thus, in the local Chinese variety one can ask *Shei-men lai-le?* 'Which people have arrived?'. In the corresponding standard Chinese expression *men* cannot be used (Baki 2012). See also 11.8.5.

An interesting selective copy of a non-Chinese phonological feature is the drop of tones in some local varieties of Chinese. In a tone language, words can be distinguished by differences in tones (Yip 2002). Chinese is clearly a tonal language, whereas Uyghur is a non-tonal language. When speaking Chinese, Uyghur speakers carry over their non-tonal habits, thus the Mandarin word *wǎngbā* for 'internet cafe' is pronounced without tone as *wangba* (Baki 2012: 49).

3 Arabic

Arabic belongs to the Semitic languages and is thus close to Hebrew and Aramaic. Like Chinese, it possesses its own script system. Arabic has developed into an appointed religious language, whose features are actually taken over in all other languages in the whole Muslim world. Even many languages outside Islam have, for cultural reasons, taken over words from Arabic, e.g. English *sugar, cotton, magazine, algebra, alcohol*.

Most countries that use Arabic as their official language are situated in the Middle East. Arabic is the official language of Algeria, Bahrain, Comoros, Chad, Djibouti, Egypt, Eritrea, Iraq, Jordan, Kuwait, Lebanon, Libya, Mauritania, Morocco, Oman, Palestine, Qatar, Western Sahara, Saudi Arabia, Somalia, Sudan, Syria, Tunisia, United Arab Emirates, and Yemen. It is also a national language in Mali and Senegal. Consequently, spoken Arabic includes numerous varieties, e.g. Standard Arabic, Egyptian Arabic, Gulf Arabic, Maghrebi Arabic, and Levantine Arabic. All these varieties exhibit rather different linguistic features.

Arabic has influenced the absolute majority of Turkic languages. These have, for example, taken over global copies of a high number of Arabic lexemes. Many varieties used in the Ottoman empire took over large-scale lexical materials from Arabic. Turkic literary languages such as those of Ottoman and Chaghatay took over incredibly versatile amounts of lexical and syntactic material.

Arabic philosophy of the 9th–12th centuries became very important for Christian Europe. It prevented a loss of important results of Western philosophy through translation of Arabic philosophical texts into Latin. Spanish is a Romance language evolving from colloquial spoken Latin in the Iberian Peninsula. It had developed from several dialects of Vulgar Latin after the collapse of the Western Roman Empire in the 5th century. The oldest Latin texts with traces of Spanish are known from Iberia in the 9th century. After establishing the Middle East and North Africa as the foundation of their new empire, the Arabs in the 8th century landed in Spain, where they continued to elaborate their language. They had great influence on the history and way of life in that part of Europe. Their kinds of science passed through the Iberian Peninsula to the remainder of Europe. The Arabs stayed in Spain for some 800 years and spent much effort to keep their language pure and free from elements taken over from other language. On the other hand, a whole range of scientific and technical words and terms were copied from Arabic. From the eight to the twelfth centuries, Arabic emerged as a full-fledged scientific language. Anyone who desired to advance in the learned world had to study and learn it. As in our days English opens the door to technical and scientific advancement, just this was the case with Arabic in the medieval period, at a time when Europe still was in the middle of the Dark Ages. By the time, the Arabs developed into masters of Spain. Arabic was well on its way to becoming the scientific language. It became the principal language of the center and the south of the Iberian Peninsula.

Latin, however, held its accustomed place in the Christian North. This situation continued until the Arabs were pushed out of Andalusia.

Spoken vulgar Latin, the ancestor of modern Spanish, consisted of four principal dialects: Mozarabic, spoken by the Christians who lived under Muslim rule and which became the principal medium for passing Arabic words into Spanish, Aragonese in Aragon and Navarre, and Leonese in Leon, which heavily took over Arabic words, and Castilian, which evolved to become the national language of Spain. An interesting copy is the global and combinational copy of the Arabic article *al*, which is found, among others, in toponyms such as *Almonaster*, where *al* is added to Latin *monasterium* (Rorabaugh 2010: 14). Rorabaugh gives a number of interesting examples of different types of copies.

4   Russian

The Russian language today possesses an overwhelming power and non-Russian first speakers in Russian-dominated areas accept its high prestige. Russian has taken over lexical items from all of the non-Russian languages of the area. On the other hand, non-Russian speakers who used Russian as a language of communication carried over elements from their first languages into Russian and created new varieties. A well-known example is the so-called *govorka*, a Russian lingua franca on the Taimyr peninsula and in the North Yenisei area, both multilingual areas with speakers of Samoyedic, Turkic (Dolgan), and Tungusic. Non-Russian combinational properties characterize the syntax, e.g. (30).

(30) Carried over syntactic features in Govorka
 Menja šaman   kostjum   odel   ego.
 I   shaman   clothing   dress-PAST   3SG
 'He dressed in my shamanic clothing.'

Example 30, shows an SOV ordering and a subject representant pronoun *ego* on the verbal predicate (Wurm 1996: 84). Combinational and semantic properties of postpositions have been copied on the Russian noun *mesto*, which is used in *govorka* as a postposition to indicate instrument, comitative dative, destination, with some other functions, see (31) (Xelimskij 1996).

(31) Carried over postpositional function in Govorka
 a. *Tebja koliti nožik mesto.*
    you   hit   knife POSTP
    Literally 'You hit knife with' meaning 'You hit it with a knife'.

b. *Gorod mesto usol.*
  town POSTP go-PAST3SG
  'X went to town.'

Xelimskij adds: "The rules of its [*govorka*'s] grammar are precise and stable (unless a speaker's language belongs to the 'post-pidgin continuum', i.e. is influenced by standard Russian)" (1996: 1034).

It is, however, hard to reconstruct Russian in its incipient stage in older times. For instance, it is well known that Swedish Vikings, in the 10th century, traded on the big Russian rivers and started settlements that later became large cities such as Novgorod and Kyiv. They thus founded new states that later evolved into Russia, Ukraine, and Belarus. The mutual bonds were also dynastical. The Swedish king Rurik had started a dynasty that ruled uninterruptedly from the 8th to the 16th century. This is, for instance, described in the accounts by Saint Nestor the Chronicler (1056–1114). Even Rus', which is the old name of Russia, emanates from Swedish as the old name for Vikings from Roslagen, the name of the historical province Uppland.

CHAPTER 8

Stability

Here follow some considerations of the stability of codes that happen to have a lower prestige and how their speakers try to cope with this situation. How are the questions of linguistic humility dealt with? How to correspond to the changes? The reactions are very different.

If a new linguistic situation has started for a strongly dominated or low-ranking language, one reaction is to try to master the loss of prestige of the own language by adapting to the innovations resulting from copying. Speakers can try to do their best to be good imitators of the new trends. This attitude relates to the numerous modern languages just now influenced by English. Very often it results in cases where old and the contact-influenced models are mixed in the same texts.

The other solution is to try to find measures to perfect the lower-prestige language. This can be practiced in many ways. One way is to act adversatively, i.e. to try to strengthen the own language in order to increase its force. This attempt may not function well if normative conservative efforts are introduced. Such a control is actually seldom auspicious. Speakers avoid a language that they cannot identify as normal, very often because they fear to abuse the conservative project. There are numerous cases of this fatal type for languages of lower force.

Stability, in terms of strength and weakness, of indigenous languages is an important issue for further studies. Linguistic descriptions should pay attention to how a variety is actually used. Mosel has published several guidelines for documentary linguistics and linguistic assistance in revitalization, mentioning "purification by the replacement of loan words" as the first task in editing recorded texts (Mosel 2012). In the publication (2014: 141–142), she modifies this recommendation concerning creating texts for the communities. When speech communities want their language to become a written language and the means of instruction in primary schools, it belongs to the responsibilities of linguists to help them create it by keeping the uniqueness of their language. They must also avoid a rigid purism that would put off younger speakers. Normativeness or purism, i.e. preserving the original state of a language, often negatively effects maintenance and revitalization efforts. Purists advocate the avoidance of copies or the upholding of a regularity that cannot be implemented in reality.

How linguists and their discipline can help speech communities to adopt successful strategies for maintaining and revitalizing their languages is an important issue. A grammar of Karaim has been published in which each sentence has a typically Turkic verb-final word order. This is extremely strange for speakers who apply a typologically dominant SVO order (Csató & Johanson 2020). Such experiences demotivate people to express themselves in the recommended varieties.

A purist attitude stigmatizes a spoken copying variety as inferior or wrong. If a precontact state of the language is selected as an aim, this reduces the chances of language retention. The aim of revitalization must be to reinforce the use of the variety that is in use to some extent, or at least remembered.

Infelicitous strategies can mislead the speaker communities and even contribute to generational shift. Linguists document and reconstruct data in diachronically and typologically coherent ways. They are generally concerned with one particular language and speak of the 'language community' as their primary target, sometimes adopting a puristic approach that aims to document the 'true' language, untainted by loans and language mixing (Austin & Sallabank 2014). The wish to keep the linguistic data free from contact influences may be reflected in the efforts of speaker communities to purify their variety. But if a language is endangered, this may really also threaten its survival (Csató 1998).

CHAPTER 9

High-Copying Codes

1   Examples of High-Copying Languages

The examples chosen here are two Turkic languages spoken in the eastern parts of Europe, on the periphery of the Turkic-speaking world, Gagauz in the Balkans, and Northwest Karaim in the Baltic area. Gagauz and Northwest Karaim have undergone profound typological changes as a result of frame-changing take-over copying.

Northwest Karaim, the Karaim language spoken in present-day Lithuania, is a Kipchak Turkic language which has been dominated by non-Turkic languages during its six-hundred-year long presence in the Circum-Baltic area in relative isolation from cognate Turkic languages. As a result of its asymmetric sociolinguistic situation, Northwest Karaim has become congruent to the dominating non-Turkic varieties, though without changing its inherited genealogical blueprint. This language can serve to illustrate a high-copying language, one that has changed under long-lasting and intensive dominance of genealogically and typologically distant languages. Some examples of what has changed, and just as important what has not changed, will give a picture of this so often misunderstood language type.

Code-Copying in Northwest Karaim is take-over copying from non-Turkic contact languages. The copies represent all types of global and selective copies. The contact-induced processes have been triggered of the speakers' need to make Karaim and the other languages of the multilingual speakers intertranslatable and create isomorphisms facilitating their use. The copies of model elements have been inserted into the Karaim Basic Code and accommodated to it. This implies that principles of the Turkic Basic Code have determined the processes as typical in take-over copying. One illustrative example is the phonological system. As mentioned, the consonant system has been extended with copied palatalized consonants. The vowel system has remained conservative preserving the front rounded vowels *ö* and *ü* and maintaining the Kipchak retarded realization of front vowels, *ó* and *ú*, in non-initial position, as e.g. in Crimean Tatar. The Turkic principle of syllabic harmony, i.e. the tendency to obligatorily classify syllables as either front or back, is realized. In Northwest Karaim, front vowels together with palatalized consonants signal front syllables and back vowels together with non-palatalized consonants signal back syllables. The principle is the same as in most other Turkic languages, the difference being that in Karaim, as a result of the copied palatalized series of consonants, all consonants can have signal function. Thus, the realization of the principle has changed; compare *K'el'-ä-b'iz'* 'We come' to *Al-a-bïz* 'We take'. The proposal forwarded by some linguists (e.g. Nevins & Vaux 2004) that Northwest Karaim has consonant harmony, is misconceived from a Turkic linguistic perspective. There are a number of valid arguments against the theoretical construct of a Karaim consonant harmony, but here I want to emphasis the evidence of Code-Copying. Such a deviation from native principles would be plausible if it were the result of a substrate influence, i.e. a carry-over copy. However, no substrate language observing consonant harmony has ever been present in the area. Consonant harmony is in any case a very infrequent phenomenon. Thus, Northwest Karaim syllabic harmony is genuinely Turkic in borrowed garments.

Northwest Karaim has changed its syntactic typological properties in a conspicuous way. Its basic SOV word order has changed to free/SVO order. As mentioned above, SVO word order occurs also in non-copying Turkic as a marked order. As a result of copying the high frequency of SVO word order in contact languages, this order has lost its markedness in Karaim. The same applies for possessive constructions. The Turkic order is genitive attribute + possessed. The genitive attribute can move to other positions, observing some restrictions (Csató 2011). As a result of convergence to non-Turkic, the restrictions in Northwest Karaim have been relaxed and the frequency of a postposed genitive attribute increased. The snow-ball effect of the word order changes has led to the use of right-branching finite embedded clauses replacing the left-branching Turkic non-finite embedded clause type.

What has not changed in this high-copying language? The morphology including the elaborated Turkic system of verbal inflection is not significantly reduced (Csató 2012). The category of the Turkic type of evidentiality is lacking as in many other peripheral Turkic languages. Prepositions have not replaced postpositions even if foreign postpositions occur in globally copied phrases. Strategies applied for copying of verbs is language specific. Several Turkic languages copy nominal forms of the foreign verb and combine it with an auxiliary functioning as the morphological base for inflection, i.e. for anchoring the copy into the Turkic grammatical frame. This strategy is used in Northwest Karaim, e.g. *zvont' et'-* 'to call' ⇐ Slavic *zvonit'*.

The lexicon contains a high number of copied lexical elements. In the Polish dominated variety, copies from Polish, in the Russian dominated variety, copies from Russian, and in the Lithuanian dominated variety, copies from Lithuanian are prevalent. Multilingual speakers can switch between these varieties. The basic vocabulary is Turkic. For instance, kinship terms denoting core family relations are Turkic, whereas non-core relations tend to be global take-over copies, e.g. *tötä* 'aunt', *dädä* 'uncle', *dvoyunarodnïy* 'cousin', and *semya* 'family name'.

Gagauz is an Oghuz Turkic language also on the western periphery of the Turkic world. The contact-induced changes in Gagauz have led to similar changes as in Northwest Karaim. The two Turkic languages belong to two different branches of Turkic, their morphology exhibits these genealogical differences. Typologically, as a result of contact-induced changes, they have become more similar (Csató & Menz 2018).

2　Attitudes towards High-Copying Varieties

Relationships between high-copying and weak purified varieties are of interest. The impact of an increasingly dominant language onto a dominated language tends to involve a massive influx of non-native forms from the dominant language. There is a high amount of structural diffusion, reinforcement of forms and patterns shared with the dominant language and loss of forms or patterns absent from the dominant language (Aikhenvald 2020: 254). Language endangerment and impending language shift may result in dialect leveling, creating new mixed, or 'blended' languages. This does not imply that copying processes themselves lead to obsolescence. Johanson (2002b) argues that structural changes in a language do not lead to 'structuritis', i.e. endangerment. Speakers shift to the dominating language when the primary code ceases to have a communicative function. The acquisition of code-copying strategies may facilitate the maintenance of communication skills in lesser used or endangered codes. The world is full of examples of successful high-copying varieties, both large and small languages such as English and Gagauz.

The difference between strongly and weakly normed languages is important. An obstacle to learning and using a high-copying variety of a language should not be imposed. It is common for people in the world to speak several varieties of a language.

It is a fact, often overlooked, that even minority and endangered languages have several varieties. Depending on the given communication situation, Turkish speakers in Germany may, for example, use a high-copying or low-copying variety of Turkish. It is the communicative functionality of a language that keeps it alive. High-copying varieties are instrumental to motivating young bilingual Turkish speakers to use Turkish when communicating with their bilingual peers. In situations where the other participant, e.g. the grandmother, is a monolingual Turkish speaker, they use a low-copying variety (Johanson 1991b).

The acquisition of competence in a high-copying variety can pave the way for the acquisition of a low-copying variety. Suppose that a Russian-speaking Karaim says (32).

(32) Northwest Karaim
Tuvχan k'ün'ün'b'ä pozdravlat' et'äb'iz.
born day-POSS2SG-POSTP.with congratulate-INTR-1PL
'We congratulate you on your birthday'

The speaker uses a copy of the Russian word for 'to congratulate', because s/he does not know the Karaim word for it. If copying is not accepted, the speaker must change the language and switch to Russian. The replacement of the verb *pozdravlat'* through the corresponding Karaim word is a trivial matter.

The complexity of multilingual skills is poorly understood. It is therefore often viewed in an over-simplistic way. The role of copying in language maintenance must be taken into account by linguists engaged in safeguarding them.

CHAPTER 10

Cognates and Copies

This chapter raises the question how distinctions between copies and cognates can be treated in the framework of the Code-Copying Model. The special case of so-called Altaic verb derivational markers will illustrate some lines of argumentation.

The term 'cognate' refers to a morpheme which is related to a morpheme in another language by virtue of inheritance from a common ancestral morpheme, whereas a copy is a morpheme taken over or carried over from a model code. The question how to distinguish between inheritance and copying is especially relevant for analyzing correspondences of bound morphology shared by two or more languages. In search for the historical causes that have given rise to these shared properties, two possibilities must be considered. The correspondences are either *inheritance*, which creates a residue of morphological similarities in daughter languages after their separation from an ancestral language, or *contact*, which leads to the copying of a bound morpheme from a model language into a basic language. The difference in the ease of copying between grammar and lexicon and between copying bound and free morphemes explains why bound morphology is held to be one of the most fruitful parts of language structure when it comes to the distinction between copies and cognates.

What are the constraints, the manifestation and the motivation of code-copying as opposed to inheritance? Why do cognate languages have bound morphology in common? Scholars contributing to the volume Johanson & Robbeets (2012) used the Code-Copying Model as a theoretical framework for answering these questions. The main issues pointed out by them are the following.

Two or more languages have bound morphology in common when their affixes share certain properties, either globally, including form and function, or selectively, restricted to certain structural—material, semantic, combinational, or frequential—properties only. What holds for linguistic similarities in general, irrespective of whether they involve lexical, phonological or grammatical correspondences, also holds for bound morphology shared between languages. There are four different ways of accounting for correspondences: chance, universals, inheritance, and code-copying. Chance has caused the formal and functional resemblance, for instance, between the future tense marker *ϑa* in Modern Greek and in the Bantu language Etsako, as was pointed out by Joseph (2012: 153). Some shared structural properties may have developed 'naturally' and thus independently in each of the languages. Universal implicational relations are known to underlie the correlation for instance between adpositions and verb position.

1 Distinctions between Cognates and Copies

There are good reasons for focusing on the distinction between copies and cognates, and only pay peripheral attention to the other determinants of morphological similarity. The observation that whereas chance and linguistic universals lead to the independent development of shared features in each of the languages, inheritance and code-copying involve a dependent development. Inheritance and code-copying generate similarities that reflect a certain historical interrelationship between the languages concerned, either through common ancestorship or through language contact. Therefore, the distinction between copies and cognates is of particular interest to the comparative historical linguist, who studies languages with connected histories.

What is likely to be inherited and what is likely to be copied? Stability refers to the likelihood of an item to be inherited. It is the tendency to resist both internally and externally motivated change rather successfully. Copiability has to do with externally motivated change only. It refers to the likelihood of an item to be affected by copying. The assumption is that a word class, a category or a part of language structure is more likely to be copied, if it is copied more frequently in cross-linguistic sampling, in other words, if they are attractive for copying.

What do cognates look like and what do copies look like? By comparing copying patterns with genealogical patterns in a cross-linguistic sample of languages, some guidelines on how to identify the effects of contact vs. inheritance in shared morphology can be formulated. For instance, globally shared morphemes are more likely to be accounted for by inheritance than by code-copying. When shared bound morphemes are restricted to shared roots only, this is an indication that they are copied rather than inherited. A good indication of genealogical continuity is shared stem alternation. The same is true for shared affix alternation. Indicative of copying is the limited distribution of morphemes within a particular contact zone. Examples of copied morphology suggest that if bound morphemes are copied at all, it is often the case that more than one form is copied. For detailed argumentations see the ingenious contributions in Johanson & Robbeets eds. (2012). See also below the implementation of some principles in the discussion on Altaic verb derivation.

2   Motivations for Copying Bound Morphemes

Why is a bound morpheme copied? The motivation for copying a bound morpheme is often an interplay of structural and social factors. When the structural motivation is strong enough, bound morphemes may be copied even in the absence of strong social pressure. Conversely the presence of a strong social motivation can ultimately foster morphological copying even in case of low structural attractiveness; cf. Comrie's introduction (2002) to Johanson (2002c).

Among the structural motivations one finds equivalence, morphotactic, morphosyntactic and mapping transparency, and semantic specificity. Morphotactic transparency obtains when the morphological segmentation of an affix is easily perceivable. Morphosyntactic transparency obtains when the grammatical function of a morpheme can be understood without considering the context of its broader morphosyntactic environment. Mapping transparency refers to a straightforward relationship between a morpheme and its meaning. Semantic factors govern global copying, frequency of use governs selective copying, as highly frequent elements are strongly entrenched in memory, and, therefore, in a position to impose themselves on speakers when these are speaking the basic language.

It is important to point out the strong impact of social factors in morphological copying. Among these factors we find dominance of the model language, duration, intensity and variety of contact, history, degree, and variety of multilingualism, and intentionality of language planning.

3   Cognates and Copies in Altaic Verb Derivation

As an example of the problems implied in discerning cognates from copies some short remarks concerning possible vestiges of common Altaic verb derivation will be presented. The common derivational markers in question have been reconstructed on the basis of Turkic, Mongolic, Tungusic, Korean, and Japanese data in order to establish arguments for the postulated Altaic genealogical relatedness of these languages.

The etymological investigation into the deverbal markers was initiated by Ramstedt (1912), who documented the vestiges of what he assumed to be the original Altaic system of deverbal stem formation. Later on, Poppe (1973) reconstructed eight markers of diathesis, citing rich Turkic, Mongolic and Tungusic material. Finally, Miller (1982, 1983) added a number of cognates found in Japanese and Korean.

Possible candidates for cognateness also include old markers of deverbal nouns, in particular the so-called aorist, mostly reconstructed as *{-ra}, e.g. Even *emu-re-m* 'I have brought'. Menges (1943) first demonstrated its importance for Altaic comparative linguistics on the basis of Tungusic data. The Turkic form, with which it is compared, is present in all Turkic languages—contrary to an assumption often repeated also in Chuvash, namely in the so-called 'future', e.g. *Vul-ă-p* 'I will read' (Johanson 1976). For Mongolic, see Menges (1968: 130–131); for Japanese and Korean, see Miller (1996: 163–168).

How to judge these reconstructions? It is true that some of them, particularly in Ramstedt's work, raise problems and that the semantics is in some cases too vague to be convincing. On the other hand, it seems hard to explain the attested data of verbal morphology in all these languages without hypothesizing the existence of a common origin. According to Miller, copying is excluded, "once we inspect the forms and their functions within the morphology" (1991a). Erdal, however, finds much of what Ramstedt and Poppe have to say in this domain "quite unacceptable", since these authors "not only fail to sort out evident recent borrowings, but often stretch semantics to suit their theory and deal with modern evidence on a par with Old Turkic" (Erdal 1997: 234). According to Doerfer, even the Turkic and Mongolic verb systems are very distant from each other: typologically and probably also genealogically separated by a world (1967: 63).

It should be borne in mind that comparative work concerns elements inherited from an original that is itself *lost*. Comparative linguistics is by definition hypothetical, since it must go beyond the oldest known linguistic records. The hypothetical constructs are necessary instruments that do not present any 'danger', if they are based on attested forms of the languages under comparison and free from contradictions in themselves as well as in their relation to other known linguistic facts. The reconstruction of proto-forms ideally depends on semantically, phonetically, morphologically, chronologically and geographically flawless correspondences. The comparison of complex words and parts of words presupposes knowledge of the word structures represented in the languages compared. In order to define derivations, which we are concerned with here, the comparatist must identify both the stems and the derivational devices.

4   Copies

Linguistic interrelations within the Altaic world are highly complex. The study of similarities and differences must also take numerous older and more recent areal interactions into account. If two languages display two units of *prima facie* similarity, one of these units may be a contact-induced global copy of the other (Johanson 1992: 15–17) and thus go back to a foreign original grammar. It is important to find criteria by means of which these so-called 'borrowings' may be identified and excluded from further genealogical comparison.

While comparative and contact-linguistic research thus complement each other, their results are profoundly different. This fact is blurred by the frequent claim that differences between genealogically related and copied units are only gradual, and that strong contacts may lead to relatedness. Copying is the imitation of one language by another and must be sharply distinguished from purely internal development.

It is, however, often ignored that the conditions in which units may be copied require as differentiated considerations as questions of genealogical relatedness. Simplistic solutions must be avoided in both cases. Linguistic elements are not handed around haphazard across languages. Copying is far from random, but rather subject to specific restrictions. Nevertheless, similarities that cannot be explained according to strict comparative criteria, e.g. similar case suffixes in Altaic languages, are often rather generously declared as contact-induced, with sweeping references to 'borrowing'. Conjuring tricks performed with copied morphemes are not necessarily less simplistic than uncritical attempts at genealogical reconstructions.

5   Evidence

What about the criteria for cognates and the criteria for copies in Altaic? A good deal of comparatively relevant regularities has been demonstrated by so-called pro-Altaicists, and many of them are also recognized by non-Altaicists. Doerfer stresses the value of the correspondences established by Ramstedt: "We must be grateful to the ingenious founder of Altaistics as a science for discovering so many sound laws which are valid to this date" (Doerfer 1985: 135). At least, numerous details make it difficult to maintain the opinion that the similarities of the Altaic languages are exclusively due to copying.

But the situation is far from unequivocal. It is therefore important that the principles and axioms established so far are further discussed and that the criteria employed are scrutinized with respect to their value as conclusive or circumstantial evidence. In discussing comparative evidence, it is important to distinguish cases in which a given comparison is

(i)   conclusively proven to be valid;
(ii)   conclusively proven to be invalid;

(iii) not proven to be valid, but supported by positive circumstantial evidence;
(iv) not proven to be valid, and not supported by positive circumstantial evidence.

These elementary distinctions are often ignored. The last two cases (iii–iv) may of course not be mistaken for the first case (i) = proof. But it is equally incorrect to deal with them as if they represented the second case (ii) = disproof. Lack of evidence is not tantamount to counter-evidence. It leads to an intellectually unsatisfactory and practically unfruitful situation if, on the one hand, absence of conclusive evidence is assessed as counter-evidence and, on the other hand, inference from known facts that are otherwise hard or impossible to explain remains unrecognized.

6   Arguments from Silence

In the specific case of derivational systems, we may say that safe reconstructions require that both stems and suffixes are attested. On the other hand, lack of this evidence does not necessarily invalidate a given reconstruction. In particular, arguments from silence based on lack of East Old Turkic evidence are not conclusive. The fact that a unit is not attested in East Old Turkic derivation as mirrored in the records available to us does not mean that it is irrelevant under a comparative aspect. Its absence does not mean absence at earlier stages of development.

It is true that in a synchronic description of the East Old Turkic derivation system "a single verb does not make a formation" (Erdal 1991: 477). Thus, *aδru-* 'to excel' cannot be derived from *aδ°r-* 'to separate', since evidence for a productive deverbal suffix {-U-} is lacking in the corpus. But this fact does not invalidate Ramstedt's etymological hypothesis concerning a corresponding Altaic type of derivation (Johanson 1994b). The grammar that has motivated the original etymology of the complex stem is not at work in the East Old Turkic word-formation system. Compare correspondences such as Japanese *tar-* 'to be sufficient', 'to be full' → *taš-* 'to fill up', with Altaic $*l_1 > r$ and $*l_2 > š$, and East Old Turkic *tol-* 'to be full' → *toš* 'to fill up', 'to make complete' with $*l_1 > l$ and $*l_2 > š$ (Miller 1996: 142–143).

The reason why we cannot rule out all phenomena lacking in the East Old Turkic corpus is not only the limited extent of this corpus. The grammar found there can, in principle, never be identical with the motivating original grammar of the putative Altaic derivations, which must be thousands of years older.

7 Copies and Copiability

To be able to discriminate between cognates and copies, comparatists have tried to establish, on empirical grounds, general tendencies with respect to the susceptibility of lexemes to copying. Similar observations are possible concerning the copiability of other elements, e.g. bound units. Certain units are more readily copied than others. This fact suggests that two comparable units are more likely to be akin in origin if they represent types that are known to be impervious to copying. Comparative Altaistics should thus pay attention to materially and semantically similar units of this kind.

Although bound morphemes often undergo special processes of analogy, similarities in certain derivational and grammatical suffixes may represent a special value for genealogical comparison. In the verbal flexion, suffixes closest to the primary stem, markers of actionality and diathesis, seem relatively little susceptible to copying. It would be a strong clue to a common origin if this 'intimate' part of verbal morphology exhibited systematic correspondences of materially and semantically similar morphemes within congruent combinational patterns.

8 Superstable Morphology?

In Johanson (1992) it is suggested that the suffixes closest to the primary verb stem might be the part of Turkic morphology that is most resistant to copying and recommended an examination of them in search of genuine correspondences between the Altaic languages. The arguments presented supports Thomason's criticism of the "superstable morphology hypothesis" (1980):

> ... even within the set of individual affixes, there are striking differences, with those most liable to copying being those that are most peripheral, such as the [...] case suffixes and person-number suffixes.
>   By contrast, the suffixes standing closest to the stem of a Turkic verb, namely those expressing actionality and diathesis, are the most impervious to copying. In this way, one can establish degrees of attractiveness independent of social factors. [...]
>   Turning to the controversy surrounding the external genealogical relations of Turkic languages within Altaic, Johanson (1992) suggests that the conservatism of Turkic verb structure—stable even in a de-Turkicized a language as Karaim—and in particular the extreme resistance to copying of the positions closest to the verb, might provide a more reliable tool than

any of those used in the past to test whether there are indeed shared elements that testify to genealogical relatedness, rather than intensive and long-lasting language contact, among the groups of languages that would constitute Altaic. (Thomason 1980).

9 Typological Arguments

Typological similarities can certainly not prove relatedness. But does this mean that structural arguments are totally out of place? Comparative research is rightly based on strict correspondences of units with certain common material and semantic properties. It is widely assumed that structural features are copied easily from language to language and that purely typological similarities thus cannot provide any conclusive evidence for genealogical issues. As a result, common structural patterns are mostly completely disregarded in current discussions on comparative issues of the Altaic languages: "The overall syntactic parallels and similarities among all the Altaic languages are so great and so immediately striking that—in a curious variety of the logic of inverse argumentation—they are, today at least, virtually never mentioned in any of the literature, whether pro- or anti-Altaic" (Miller 1991b: 308).

As already stated, contact-induced copying processes should not be less strictly argued for than genealogical connections. If the common structural features of the Altaic languages are studied in an accurate and differentiated way, with due attention to the interplay of structural and social factors, it might well turn out that at least some of the typological correspondences provide strong arguments against copying and give positive circumstantial evidence in favor of genealogical connections. As regards the verbal systems, there are, for example, common patterns in the use of so-called causative morphemes such as *{-bu:-}, which may be interpreted both as 'causatives' ('to let do') and as 'passives' ('to be done'), without being identical with any of them. These markers actually signal the semantic notion of 'transcendence' in the sense that the range of the action transcends the domain of the first actant, which is either the source or the goal of the action. This semantic notion is grammaticalized in several Altaic languages; for Turkic, see Johanson (1974, 1998a: 55–56), for Even {-w-}, see Benzing (1955: 48), for 'reversives' in Japanese, Korean, etc., see Miller (1982, 1996: 126).

CHAPTER 11

Types of Copying in Written Languages

On the basis of examples from the world of written letters, the present chapter provides a general overview over phenomena describable as 'written language intertwining', i.e. high-copying written languages. The question is how the phenomena are realized and how they interrelate from a contact-linguistic point of view. It appears that they mostly represent ways of writing in which a specific genre requires some kind of interwining. They thus mostly concern texts rather than concerning languages.

The phenomena are of dual nature, displaying elements from at least two different historical sources. They arise in bilingual settings as a result of marked language contact. The relative prestige of the interacting codes is an important factor. The phenomena concern the relations between higher-ranking and lower-ranking codes. The intertwining usually concerns matters of linguistic 'purity' as opposed to kinds of 'hybridity'. Writers and readers may possess very different degrees of competence in the codes involved. Lower-ranking codes may be used to secure wide accessibility of a message, e.g. of religious and political teachings. Some types have specific functions in different domains: literature, religion, administration, trade, etc. They often acquire particular stylistic functions, dictated by conventions of certain genres. A more prestigious code may serve as a kind of tutor or mentor to a less prestigious code. Efforts to keep the higher-ranking codes 'pure' are often undermined by phenomena of intertwining. Scribal traditions and their degrees of strictness are important factors. Scribal traditionalism may produce more or less 'artificial' results, e.g. alloglottography, the use of a written language different from the language of utterance.

The phenomena are rather different and thus do not constitute a uniform class. Their definitions have mostly lacked precision and clear demarcations of the relevant types. In general, they have been rather neglected in the linguistic literature. Their study is theoretically and empirically much more controversial than the study of spoken varieties as dealt with in the literature on so-called mixed spoken languages, e.g. in Bakker & Mous (1994) or in Matras & Bakker (2003), and the discussions about them have been characterized by even more confusion. Since written or literary languages are often engineered in partly 'artificial' ways, e.g. through measures of language policy, they may be expected to display contact-linguistic features different from those observed in more natural languages. Many interesting questions will be left open here, e.g. the influence of the types of script system on the different kinds of intertwining.

What do the phenomena have in common? They arise in bilingual settings as a result of marked language contact. They are of dual nature, displaying elements from two different historical sources, elements derivative of two linguistic codes. None represents mixing in the sense of a random or untidy collection of dissimilar elements or an indiscriminate confusion that would make it in principle impossible to distinguish the individual elements.

The relative prestige of the interacting codes is an important ingredient. The phenomena concern the relation between higher-ranking and lower-ranking codes. The former are dominant, more prestigious, the latter are dominated, less prestigious. The sociolinguistic rating grades high 'high(er)' and low 'low(er)' will be used to indicate them. Higher-ranking codes are culturally dominant mainstream codes, superior in authority, influence, and/or status. They are cultured, ceremonial, cultic, administrative, scientific, literary varieties, official standards, hegemonial, colonial languages, lingua francas, and sometimes international superstandards such as Latin, Arabic or today's English. On the use of Latin in Sweden see Helander (2004). Lower-ranking codes are often vernaculars, nonstandard varieties, local dialects, more limited native varieties of a country or a region, sometimes nonstandard varieties of global languages. Higher-ranking codes are not linguistically superior to the corresponding lower-ranking ones, and they are not always politically superior to them. Their common feature is their higher cultural prestige in specific historical situations.

The phenomena to be dealt with are of five types:
(i) Take-over copying from a higher-ranking Model Code.
(ii) Carry over copying from into a higher-ranking Basic Code.
(iii) Alternate use of elements of a higher ranking and a lower ranking code.
(iv) A lower-ranking code is used to explicate texts in a higher-ranking code.
(v) Elements of a higher-ranking code are used in texts to represent a lower-ranking code.

The five types may be exemplified with the roles of Latin, once the dominant written language in Western Europe, and so-called vernaculars such as Italian and German, used in the early history of European literature.
1. Copies from Latin are taken over in a written vernacular.
2. Copies from a vernacular are carried over to a variety of Latin.
3. Latin and vernacular elements alternate in texts.
4. Vernacular elements are used to explicate texts in Latin.
5. Latin elements are used to represent vernacular elements.

The realization of the types dealt with here is subject to considerable variation.

The higher-ranking codes are often conservative, in some cases not genuinely living native varieties any more. They tend to be idealized, used as symbols of authority, power, wisdom, education, learning, etc., fulfilling formal and ceremonial functions. Efforts to keep them 'pure' are often undermined by phenomena of intertwining. Scribal traditions and their degrees of strictness are important factors for their development. Scribal traditionalism may produce more or less 'artificial' results. An extreme form of this is alloglottography, the use of a written language different from the language of utterance, particularly observable in old cuneiform traditions.

Writers and readers involved may have very different degrees of competence in the codes concerned.

Some types are connected with the spread of religions and other cultural movements. Some may appear as markers of cultural separateness. Lower-ranking codes may be used to secure wide accessibility of a message, e.g. of religious and political teachings. A well-known example is the use of European vernaculars, formerly under Latin hegemony, for the successful spread of religious writings in the course of the Protestant Reformation movement. Gautama Buddha preferred to teach in local languages. Sultān Veled, the son of Jelāleddīn Rūmī, used 'rough' Anatolian Turkish instead of Persian to spread the Sufi wisdom of his father in less literate circles (Johanson 1993a).

Some types have specific functions in different domains, literature, religion, administration, trade, etc. They often acquire particular stylistic functions, dictated by conventions of certain genres.

A more prestigious code may serve as a kind of tutor or mentor to a less prestigious code. This is observed in most variations of the types dealt with here.

1   Types 1 and 2: Take-over and Carry-over Copying

What is the position of Types 1 and 2 in terms of contact-induced change? They represent code copying in the sense that copies of elements of a Model Code X are inserted into a written Basic Code Y, which therewith becomes more X-like. The copying may proceed in two directions also in written codes:

Type 1.   Take-over influence. Users of a lower-ranking Basic Code take over copies of linguistic elements from a higher-ranking Model Code.

Type 2.   Carry-over influence. Users of a lower-ranking Model Code carry over copies of linguistic elements from this code to their own variety of a higher-ranking Basic Code.

In both types, features emerge that are not originally present in either of the two interacting codes. It is in principle possible to identify two 'sources', X and Y, but the resulting Basic Code does not consist of a simple combination of X-derived and Y-derived elements. Among the known written languages displaying this kind of intertwining, none seems to have arisen through fusion of two distinct languages from which they have taken their elements, equally or almost equally. One of the codes is the Basic Code, which copies elements from the other code, the Model Code. The intertwined codes are not of mixed breed: each has a single parent in the genealogical sense (cf. Dixon 1997: 11–12). If family metaphors are needed, it would be preferable to speak of relatives by marriage, i.e. step-parents.

In both Type 1 and Type 2, a code may exhibit an excessive number of copies from the other code. Not even excessive copying, however, causes languages to break away from their families and to enter new genealogical affiliations. For example, though High Ottoman displays an inordinately large admixture of conventionalized lexical copies from Arabic-Persian, it is still a Turkish variety and a member of the Turkic family. The lexicon is not a reliable diagnostic instrument for the genealogical classification. General assumptions to the effect that the basic vocabulary is resistant to copying are far from thrustworthy. Even large parts of basic vocabularies may be copied. According to a classification based on the lexicon, Ottoman sentences full of lexical elements of Arabic-Persian origin would have to be defined as non-Turkic.

This would mean a situation where the normal transmission of the language as a totality of interrelated structures has ceased to operate. More reliable instruments are morphosyntactic subsystems, e.g. features of inflectional morphology, which are less prone to replacement through copying. Thus, for instance, in Ottoman the morphology is mainly Turkish; see 11.7.3.

2   Subtypes of Type 1 Take-over Copying

In Type 1, take-over copying, copies from a higher-ranking code are inserted into texts of a lower-ranking code. The latter provides the morphosyntactic frame for the insertion. All known human languages show this behavior.

Some written codes of this kind are characterized by excessive copying. In exceptional cases they may have arisen like certain spoken languages such as Michif, which can historically be regarded as a Cree structure into which copies of French noun phrases have been inserted. Even relexification is possible, with large parts of the lexicon of a lower-ranking code being replaced by that of a higher-ranking code, though without any drastic changes to the grammar. If excessive copying is enough to define a language as mixed, written English with its heavy amount of lexical copies from Romance would be a good case in point (Jespersen 1922: 210), but, in fact, it rather represents normal contact-induced phenomena with numerous lexical copies incorporated and more or less adapted to the Basic Code. This subtype of take-over copying, which will be labeled subtype 1, does not seem to deserve to be characterized as 'mixed', or 'hybrid', even if it involves excessive copying.

Yiddish, a rich literary language written with Hebrew script, was formerly described as a mixed language. Baumgarten mentions such claims whose echoes were still detectable up to the 19th and 20th centuries (2005: 14–15). Zunz characterized Yiddish a hybrid and composite dialect (1832: 438–442). Today, nobody in the field of Yiddish linguistics would assign the language to Type 4 exhibiting an extreme grade of mixing. On the linguistic features of written Yiddish see Birnbaum (1979), Katz (1987), and Jacobs (2005).

Certain high-copying languages, however, seem to deviate from this pattern by a tendency to keep the copies separate from the native elements of the Basic Code. Elements copied from the higher-ranking code are less adapted 'foreign elements', as opposed to 'loan elements', comparable to unadapted Latin elements in older European languages, e.g. German *von den pronominibus* 'of the pronouns', with a Latin case ending (Jespersen 1922: 213), or unadapted Hebrew elements in Yiddish, e.g. *ganovim* 'thieves', with a Hebrew plural ending. The copies are thus consciously treated as a foreign layer, a distinct segregated component separated from the indigenous material, as if they still belonged to a foreign code. Such cases of compartmentalization makes it reasonable to reckon with a subtype 2. It will be exemplified below with Akkadian influence on West Semitic, Arabic influence on written New Persian, and New Persian influence on the Turkic written languages Ottoman and Chaghatay. Observe that New Persian is Persian spoken since the 8th to 9th centuries in Greater Iran in parts of Western Asia, Central Asia, South Asia, Xinjiang, and the Caucasus. It is thus not the same as Modern or Contemporary Persian, spoken from the 19th century to present.

3 Type 2: Carry-over Copying

In the case of Type 2, carry-over copying, copies from a lower-ranking code are inserted into texts in some variety of a higher-ranking code. The latter provides the morphosyntactic frame for the insertion. A bi- or multilingual group with a relatively low-ranking primary code may, for example, choose another code in their linguistic repertoire, a prestige code, as their medium of written expression.

The product deviates more or less from the standard or mainstream variety of the higher-ranking code. In the literature, the attribute 'deviant' often has pejorative or negative overtones, as if the varieties in question were corrupt or depraved. This is by no means intended here. The deviations from the mainstream variety may be a result of imperfect learning, i.e. the authors may fail to learn the more prestigious code. Imperfect literacy is often of considerable importance for the development of a cultural community. Writers may also, however, be competent users of the higher-ranking code but deliberately deviate from the mainstream version for cultural and stylistic reasons. In both cases, the resultant variety is hardly 'freewheeling', without concern for rules, as is sometimes claimed. It simply does not obey the orthodox rules of the corresponding mainstream variety. In both cases, the differences may be conventionalized and remain as substratum influence.

Type 2 will be exemplified below with Prākrit carry-over influence on non-canonical written versions of Sanskrit, Japanese influence on deviant Chinese, Mongolian influence on deviant Chinese, and Manchu carry-over influence on deviant Chinese.

4 Type 3: Alternate Use of the Codes

Groups participating in language contacts may be bi- or multiliterate, i.e. literate in more than one of the languages involved. The types of literacy created in such settings display specific phenomena of interaction.

The literature offers many examples of bi- and multiliterate texts. Linguistic and cultural contacts in the ancient world brought forth numerous written products of this kind, documented in monuments of various kinds. Two or more texts conveying the same meaning may appear at the same location, e.g. on the Rosetta Stone with parallel texts in Egyptian—in hieroglyphic and Demotic script—and classical Greek, or in the trilingual Bīsitūn inscription with cuneiform texts in Old Persian, Elamite, and Babylonian. Other inscriptions may combine different texts, e.g. a funerary inscription in one language and an epigram in another language. Numerous inscriptions of these kinds are known throughout the ancient world (Adams et al. 2002). For example, *ostraca*, pieces broken off from earthenware vessels, in Roman Egypt would contain scattered words of the higher-ranking language Greek (Fewster 2002). There are, of course, innumerable cases of simple quotations, e.g. spoken Aramaic phrases quoted in the Greek text of the New Testament.

The phenomenon that will interest us here is, however, the alternate use of two codes in one text, typical of biliterate writers. It does not represent code copying, the insertion of copies from one code into a structure of another code. It rather corresponds to code switching in spoken registers, the succession of two languages in the course of a single speech event. Unlike spontaneous speech, however, it tends to be conscious, deliberate, and planned.

Biliterate competence may supply enlarged repertoires for expressing differentiated meaning. Careful writers can take advantage of these possibilities, at least in specific genres. They address a biliterate readership that understands the function of the alternations and appreciates their stylistic value. Complex cultural, social, political, and historical factors may underlie the conscious use of two codes. Each of them may have distinct symbolic or emblematic functions. Elements of a higher-ranking code may be used as markers of prestige in texts that are largely written in a lower-ranking code. Reversely, elements of a lower-ranking code may occur in texts that are largely composed in a higher-ranking code. Writers choosing this option are often native speakers of the lower-ranking code. The choice may mark their identity and sometimes express a certain distance or even resistance to a hegemonial language. Characteristics associated with the culture connected with a lower-ranking code may lead authors to switch to it in order to describe persons or events mentioned in the text. Historically, alternation has often been a sign of incipient literacy, heralding the birth of new literary languages. Authors may initially have failed to master the lower-ranking code, or they may have hesitated to use it because it still lacked literary acceptance.

Type 3 will be exemplified below with bilingual poems, often referred to as 'macaronic', bilingual Hebrew-Romance texts, Manchu-Chinese mixed poetry, and mixed text-types in medieval British commercial writing.

5   A Lower-Ranking Code Explicates Texts in Higher-Ranking Code

A lower-ranking code may be used to explicate texts in a higher-ranking code. The results are not hybrid languages, but hybrid written styles. There are various subtypes of strategies of this kind.

What may seem to be a mixed language may thus in reality be a text in a foreign higher-ranking code with added information in a lower-ranking code, aimed at helping to read and understand the text. It is a didactic technique, a reading aid intended to resolve linguistic comprehension difficulties.

One subtype encompasses special translation techniques for elucidating the original texts. A case in point is a heavily Graecized variety of Syriac found in translations of Greek biblical, theological, and philosophical texts of the 6th–8th centuries. It has been called an 'extraordinary hybrid variety of Syriac for use in translating Greek texts', and characterized as 'perhaps the most extreme example of the influence of one language in another to be found in the ancient world' (Taylor 2002: 328). It was a deliberately chosen translation strategy for evoking the original text lying behind the translations, motivated by the need to produce authoritative Syriac texts that reflected the Greek originals accurately (Taylor 2002: 330). It is not a 'hybrid' reflecting the Syriac language of the time. Fluent bilingual writers would hardly have admitted, in normal texts, this kind of influence of the higher-ranking secondary code on the lower-ranking primary code.

Hybrid written styles of Type 4 will be exemplified below with the Japanese *kunten* annotation technique for reading and deciphering Chinese texts, Burmese reading aids for written Pali, Sinhalese reading aids for Pali texts, and Karaim word-by-word translations as a resource for literal exegesis of Hebrew texts.

6 Type 5: Higher Ranking Code as Graphic Representation of the Lower Ranking Code

A higher-ranking code may be used to represent an utterance in a lower-ranking code. There may be wide gaps between the graphic representation in the written higher-ranking code and the way the messages conveyed are read aloud.

The use of the conservative graphic system of a higher-ranking code may conceal much of the actual phonic substance of the corresponding forms in a lower-ranking code. This was, for example, the case with Ottoman Turkish, Chaghatay, and many other Islamic languages written in Arabic script.

There are, however, also far more complex and intriguing forms of gaps between the graphic representation and the corresponding spoken message. A text in one code may be dealt with *as if* it represented another code. One specific form is so-called alloglottography, whereby a text in one code is read out in another code. A given message formulated in a lower-ranking code must be recovered from a document composed in a higher-ranking code. The principles for this representation are reminiscent of the modern practice of reading *that is* for *i.e.* (Latin *id est*), *namely* for *scil.* (Latin *scilicet* < *scire licet*), *for example* for *e.g.* (Latin *exempli gratia* 'for the sake of an example'), *namely* for *viz.* (Latin *videlicet*).

Type 5 will be exemplified below with Semitic and other codes represented in cuneiform writing, Old Persian represented in Elamite writing, Middle Iranian represented in Aramaic writing, and Japanese represented in Chinese writing.

7 Examples of Type 1 Take-over Copying

7.1 *Akkadian Take-over Influence on West Semitic*

Akkadian and cuneiform were employed for administration and correspondence far beyond the limits of Mesopotamia. The native languages of the scribes sometimes influenced their usage, giving rise to features untypical of mainstream Akkadian. These deviant varieties were not necessarily the result of imperfect learning, products of scribes who failed to learn Akkadian sufficiently, but could also be deliberately chosen distinct varieties in their own right.

In spite of its designation, so-called 'Amarna Akkadian', often referred to as a mixed Kanaanite-Akkadian language, is not likely to be a variety of this kind. It is documented in a diplomatic correspondence from the middle of the 14th century BCE, in the so-called 'Amarna letters' sent to the Egyptian Pharaoh by vassal kings and provincial governors in Syria and Palestine. The letters are parts of a collection of clay tablets found in Tell el-Amarna in Egypt and first edited by Knudtzon (1907–1915). They are mostly written in Akkadian cuneiform, the writing system of ancient Mesopotamia. Linguistic studies on Amarna Akkadian include Böhl (1909), Moran (1950), Rainey (1973, 1975), Izre'el (1978, 1991, 2005), Kossmann (1989), and Gianto (1990).

The documents written in Palestine and Syria, the regions where the Kanaanite languages Hebrew and Phoenician were spoken later, do not represent a deviant variety of Akkadian into which scribes carried over copies from their West Semitic native code. They represent the ancestor of Kanaanite, which belongs to the Northwestern subgroup of the West Semitic branch and are thus composed in the oldest attested form of West Semitic. Akkadian represents the East Semitic branch, which differs in many respects considerably from West Semitic.

Most texts represent a variety dealt with by Kossmann (1989). Its orthography is a peculiar variant of the Akkadian spelling systems. It combines Akkadian lexical items with West Semitic inflectional morphemes. West Semitic features include affixes, apophony patterns, clause and sentence syntax, e.g. word order, i.e. SVO instead of Akkadian SOV. It is doubtful whether this variety was ever a spoken language. In reality, it may have been used exclusively by scribes.

'Amarna Akkadian' of this kind is probably not a 'West-Semitized' East Semitic variety (Kossmann 1989). The Basic Code was West Semitic, into which lexical copies from the higher-ranking Akkadian code were inserted. Though the cuneiform system conceals most of the phonic substance, the lexical copies were obviously treated as a segregated component, which makes this variety a candidate for a subtype of take-over. With respect to the treatment of the lexical material, there are similarities to Type 5, in which a higher-ranking code is used to represent a lower-ranking code.

7.2 Arabic Take-over Influence on New Persian

Many Iranian languages have been deeply influenced by Semitic. The first one to be massively affected by Arabic was New Persian. Arabic was the first language of Islam, the original medium by which the new religion was established over a huge geographic area. It replaced Middle Persian as the administrative language of the Iranian-speaking world in the 8th century CE. New Persian, however, started its carrier simultaneously. The Islamic conquest of Persia (633–656), which led to the end of the Sassanid Empire, marks the beginning of its upswing.

The Middle Iranian non-Islamic language Soghdian had long been used as a lingua franca along the Silk Road between China and Transoxiana. New Persian eventually took over this function in the northeastern part of the Iranian-speaking area, a region of mixed ethnic composition. It started as a koiné along the trade routes in the western part of Central Asia, a region with speakers of Iranian varieties such as Middle Persian, Parthian, Soghdian, Khwarezmian, Baktrian, and Khotanese, other Indo-European varieties such as Tokharian, and a number of Turkic varieties. It developed into a transregional lingua franca of the eastern parts of the Islamic world, a medium of inter-ethnic communication that replaced both Middle Persian and Soghdian.

New Persian is the first Islamicized language in history, i.e. it became the second language of Islam, after Arabic. It was made fit for this function by taking over an extreme amount of lexical copies from Arabic. New Persian was established as a written language by the 9th century. Within one century it developed into a consolidated written standard language fulfilling a variety of functions. This was the result of specific religious, political, and cultural circumstances. A written standard of composite character took over the role of a Muslim medium of interethnic communication. An Islamic cultural network, employing New Persian as its medium, spread geographically from the 11th century on. The language gained increasing acceptance, both as a primary code of large groups and as a secondary code of native speakers of other languages. It was used for administrative purposes, and it became the official and cultural language of numerous Islamic dynasties.

New Persian did not continue its existence as a marginal language in the shade of Arabic. It evolved into a new prestigious standard language under the hegemony of Islam. It did not reach its position as a literary and standard language in opposition to Arabic, but as a functionally complementary tool. There was a division of tasks between written Arabic and written New Persian. Certain domains, theology, philosophy, and related sciences, were originally reserved for Arabic. Persian literature—narrative prose, epics, and poetry—enjoyed high prestige and a popularity that supported the spread of the language. The works of Firdousī, Nizāmī, and others became models for literatures far beyond the New Persian area. Other important Islamic literary languages were established according to this pattern of Islamicization, in particular Ottoman Turkish, Chaghatay, and Urdu, which emerged, as it were, as cultural 'daughter languages' of New Persian. On New Persian as an Islamic and Arabic-influenced language see Utas (2004) and Fragner (2006).

Certain linguistic properties made New Persian suited for this career. It was based on Sasanian Middle Persian, albeit simplified and refashioned, comprising elements from other varieties of the region. Its morphology was reduced compared to Middle Persian. The nominal inflection system was scanty, and the verbal system had a simple structure.

Written New Persian was profoundly influenced by Arabic. The use of the Arabic script had a high symbolic value, clearly identifying the language as Islamic. The language was unlimitedly open for copies of Arabic lexical elements and thus totally reshaped. By the 12th century, almost half of the vocabulary was Arabic-derived. The semantics of native Iranian words was influenced. Numerous copies were created, e.g. *namāz* 'ritual worship', *rūza* 'fast(ing)', or the names of the times of prayer. Arabic grammar became the model for scholarly attempts to analyze New Persian. The main interest of the native grammarians was poetics and lexicography on Arabic patterns, a continuation of the old *frahang* (New Persian *farhang*) tradition. The Arabic metrical system was applied to Persian poetry (Johanson & Utas 1994, Johanson 1994a). Domestic lexicography focused on words used in poetry, e.g. on inventories of possible rhyme words, a legacy from Arabic philology (Utas 2004).

Though New Persian copied excessively from Arabic, it is not a hybrid in the sense of a mixed breed, a fusion of two source languages that cannot be classified as belonging to either of the language families. The excesses did not lead it to break away from its family and to enter a new glossogenetic process. It remained an Iranian language, a genealogical descendant of Indo-European, not of Semitic. Arabic is not a 'parent', but rather, as it were, a 'step parent'. To continue the old outworn biological metaphors, the connection is thus not 'by blood', but rather 'by marriage'. With another metaphor, Arabic could be said to act as a kind of tutor or mentor to New Persian. It was a strong lexifier, from which a substantial part of the lexicon was copied, replacing much of the Iranian-derived vocabulary.

On the other hand, written New Persian is a mixed system in the sense of compartmentalization. Its large Arabic-derived element is a relatively segregated component, treated as a layer separated from the indigenous component, the distinctive feature being a low degree of adaptation to the native system. This fact makes it a representative of another subtype of take-over and a close structural counterpart of High Ottoman Turkish, even if the segregation may be less strict than in the latter.

7.3 New Persian Take-over Influence on High Ottoman

Speakers of Iranian and Turkic have been in a more than millennium-long continuous cultural interaction (Johanson & Bulut 2006, Csató et al. eds. 2016). Turkic-speaking groups early began to adopt Iranian linguistic habits. New Persian was the medium through which Turks of Central Asia were acquainted with Islam and urban forms of Islamic culture. Persian elements, including originally Arabic elements, were copied early in direct contact situations. Thus numerous copies penetrated Oghuz Turkic, the predecessor of Turkish, Azeri, and Turkmen. The term 'Arabic-Persian' will be used here for Arabic lexical elements that entered Turkic via Persian. The Turkic Islamic literary languages that emerged in the late Middle Ages were immediately subject to strong Persian impact and thoroughly influenced by the prestigious Arabic-Persian vocabulary.

The first Oghuz varieties in Anatolia are known as Early Anatolian Turkish (Mansuroğlu 1954). One variety, Ottoman Turkish, became the official language of the Ottoman empire and thus gained wide transregional validity. Its functions were expanded, and its resources were complemented by numerous elements of Arabic-Persian origin (Johanson 1989). Ottoman was the only recognized literary medium of the new state. It developed—as Middle Ottoman, from the 16th century onwards, thereafter as Late Ottoman—into the leading Turkic language, which produced an abundantly rich literature comprising a variety of forms and styles.

Ottoman as a whole was not, as is sometimes claimed, an 'artificial' Arabic-Persian hybrid language written by and for an élite, without connection to the language of the illiterate layers of the society. It displays a considerable diversity, from elaborated registers comprehensible only to a learned élite, to simple, unsophisticated registers closer to the spoken varieties.

Three registers of Ottoman were commonly distinguished by indigenous scholars: a high *fāsih türkče* 'correct or eloquent Turkish', an intermediate *orta türkče* 'middle Turkish', and a low *ḳaba türkče* 'rough, vulgar Turkish'. The less formal middle register was based on educated Istanbul speech. In the course of the centuries, it was modified by speakers of different origin, incorporating elements from various sides. It was a spoken register that was only occasionally written. It is poorly documented, since the preserved written sources mostly represent the high register.

What interests us here is this written high register, High Ottoman, which was not a standard language usable for everyday communication. It was thoroughly immersed in the prestigious tradition of Islamic high culture, accessible to persons with a solid knowledge of New Persian. The mass of users of Ottoman would only master a small portion of its vocabulary, in more or less adapted forms. High Ottoman was used for florid, ornate written styles, providing a remarkable wealth of expressive resources and stylistic refinement. From the latter part of the 15th century on, refined registers emerged, tailored for official correspondence and élite literature and overloaded with Arabic-Persian elements, for instance, the highly elaborated literary style known as *inšā* 'composition'.

Ottoman-Turkish poetry was essentially modeled on Persian poetry in style, diction, and meter, only slightly adapted to the requirements of the native language. It was extremely absorptive as regards Arabic-Persian lexical elements, but the claim that Ottoman poetry, as a whole, looks like an immense corpus of *mulamma* or 'macaronic' poems is clearly erroneous.

The cultivation of High Ottoman in order to strengthen its efficacy played an important role in the empire, but Ottoman as a whole was never codified systematically. Dictionaries and grammars were produced by foreigners. Ottoman grammarians largely ignored the native component, but endeavored to determine and cultivate the Arabic-Persian component, setting up rules for its vocabulary, spelling, pronunciation, and grammar. Only after the introduction of a new education system in the 19th century did the study of the Turkic element become more important.

The strength of written Ottoman increased with the power of the Ottoman empire, which culminated in the 17th century. Owing to the overwhelming mass of copied words and expressions, a deep discrepancy emerged between the high register and other registers. High Ottoman almost seemed to have lost its 'Turkic character'. The abundance of Arabic-Persian lexical elements led to strong puristic efforts in the 20th century to create a so-called *Öztürkçe* 'Pure Turkish'. The language reform drastically reduced and weakened the status of the Arabic-Persian lexical copies in modern Turkish (Lewis 1999).

What are the linguistic features of High Ottoman? Even texts overloaded with lexical copies can be clearly defined as Turkic on the basis of a native layer of lexical elements including bound morphology. Inflectional and derivational markers, most pronouns, quantifiers, and postpositions are of Turkic origin. In particular, the finite and infinite inflectional markers of the complex Turkic verb morphology, are maintained. They are typical of the Turkic agglutinative system, in which each formative in principle encodes a single category.

The lexicon contains numerous items whose structure can be analyzed within the Arabic grammar. Many are connected with each other by associative bonds and even by certain phonological-morphological correspondences, e.g. *kita:b* 'book', *ka:tib* 'clerk', 'scribe', *mektub* 'letter', *mekteb* 'school', which represent the semantic field of 'writing' on the basis of the root *K-T-B*. Correlations of this kind do not, however, allow us to establish regular correspondences with the basic Turkic-derived elements, i.e. to classify Ottoman as genealogically belonging to the Semitic family. In spite of massive copying, the Basic Code has clearly remained Turkic. As in the case of New Persian, strong and intensive contacts have not led the language to break away from its family. High Ottoman is not a fusion of source languages that leaves the question about its genealogy open (Johanson 2002a, 2002b).

An example of Ottoman prose from Evliya Çelebi's *Seyahatname* 'Book of Travels'.

(33) Ottoman prose
Xuda: 'a:lim-dir bu kadar seya:hat-de an-lar gibi jeng-a:ver
God wise-COP this much travel-LOC they like pugnacious
feta:-lar ve dil-a:ver ser veriji server-ler gör-me-di-m.
youth-PL and brave head giving chief-PL see-NEG-PAST-1SG
Dankoff's translation: 'Heaven is my witness that in all my travels I have never seen such courageous youths and pugnacious warriors as these' (1990: 213).

Of Arabic origin: *'a:lim* 'wise', 'knowing', *fetā* 'youth', 'lad', *kadar* 'amount', 'as much as', *seya:hat* 'journey', 'travel', *ve* 'and'. Of Persian origin: *dil-a:ver* 'brave', 'courageous', *jeng-a:ver* 'warrior', *ser* 'head', *Xuda:* 'God'. Of Turkic origin: *bu* 'this', {-DA} 'locative', *an-lar* 'they', *gibi* 'like', {-lAr} 'plural,' *ver-* 'to give', {-(y)iji} '-er' (agent noun), *gör-* 'to see', {-mA} 'negation'. {-DI} 'past', {-(I)m} 'I'.

The following Ottoman sentence only contains Arabic-Persian lexemes but Turkish morphology.

(34) High-copying Ottoman sentence
Bir müselles-in mesa:ha-i sathi:ye-si, ka:ide-sin-in
a triangle-GEN superficies-POSS3SG base-POSS3SG-GEN
irtifa:'-in-a ha:sïl-ï żarb-in-in nïsf-in-a
height-POSS3SG-DAT product-POSS3SG-GEN half-POSS3SG-DAT
müsa:vi:-dir.
equal-COP

'The area of a triangle is equal to the length of the base multiplied by half the height.'

The lexemes *mesāha-i sathīye* and *hāṣil-i żarb* are so-called *iżāfet* nominal constructions copied from Persian. They consist of *mesāha* 'measure', *sathī-ye* 'superficial', *hāṣil* 'result', *żarb* 'multiplication', respectively, with a connecting vowel element *-i/-ï* in between. The word *sathī-ye* 'superficial' bears an Arabic feminine suffix. The case suffix {-nIn}, third person possessive suffix {-(s)I(n)}, the dative suffix {-(y)A} and the final copula {-DIr} are Turkish.

In its modern Turkish neologistic version, the sentence has the following form containing Turkish lexemes.

(35) Standard Turkish
‹Bir üçgen-in   yüz-ölçüm-ü   taban-ın-ın
a   triangle-GEN superficies-POSS3SG base-POSS3SG-GEN
yüksekliğ-in-e   çarpım-ın-ın   yarı-sın-a
height-POSS3SG-DAT product-POSS3SG-GEN half-POSS3SG-DAT
eşit-tir.›
equal-COP

To sum up, historically, High Ottoman is a Turkic language into which thousands of copies of foreign words, even many representing the core vocabulary, were taken over. Did these lexical copies just enrich its vocabulary, or did they create some kind of mixed system? If this extraordinary hypertrophy is enough to classify the language as 'mixed', this would be equally valid for English with its abundance of lexical copies from Romance; see 7.1. This is the implication of Jespersen's comparison between English and what he simply referred to as 'Turkish' (1922: 210).

A reason why it might be justified to postulate a special mixed or dual system for written High Ottoman is the special status of the Arabic-Persian copies, which constitute a stratum consciously separated from the indigenous part of the vocabulary. They are only slightly adapted to the native system and thus show peculiarities alien to Turkish word structure, e.g. unusual phonological representations. The two components of the lexicon are strictly segregated, similar to the treatment of Arabic lexical copies in New Persian. This compartmentalization, which has much in common with the use of a foreign language, is far from typical of high-copying languages in general, e.g. of English, whose lexical elements of Romance origin show high degrees of adaptation.

The duality observed in High Ottoman makes the language a representative of subtypes of Type 1 (11.2) and a close structural counterpart of New Persian.

It is the result of a scholarly tradition. Ottoman was one of the principal languages of the Islamic cultural sphere, strongly influenced by the prestige language New Persian, and itself the prestigious language of an educated elite. It flourished at the court, in the administration, the clergy, the theological schools, the dervish orders, etc. Its architects and their followers endeavored to maintain the purity, the original form, of the copied elements. These scholars had a thorough knowledge of Arabic and Persian, a result of Ottoman education, in which reading was based on Arabic-Persian materials and texts were pronounced according to traditional rules. These conventions prevented any significant influence of the vernacular on written High Ottoman.

On the basis of these facts, Németh defined High Ottoman as a 'Mischsprache' (1953). With reference to Stalinist linguistic doctrines, he characterized the dual system as morbid or unhealthy (German 'krankhaft'). Under extraordinary social conditions, he argued, features of the language of the higher layers may overgrow. Certain literary products of the learned classes bear witness to a dual linguistic consciousness in which the foreign part is decisive and the native part is unimportant. Modern Turkey had finally overcome this dilemma through its language reforms. The foreign words had to a high degree been removed, and the foreign grammatical elements had been almost totally eliminated. Németh predicted that Turkish would face a new and healthy development owing to the fact that its grammar and its basic vocabulary had essentially remained Turkish.

Which were the specific features of the Arabic-Persian-derived elements in High Ottoman? The language had two separate phonological systems that did not influence each other essentially. Violation of sound-harmony rules was an important distinctive phenomenon of Arabic-Persian-derived elements. Foreign initial consonants, *f*-, *h*-, *l*-, *m*-, *n*-, *p*- *r*-, *š*-, *z*-, avoided in the vernacular, were permitted. Long vowels and glottal stops were pronounced as such. The Arabic-Persian copied lexemes defied certain historical sound changes that were observed in native words. The script played a conserving role. The Arabic-Persian elements were written essentially in the same way during the entire history of Ottoman, whereas native words were often subject to graphic changes and vacillations.

Though the grammar was essentially Turkic, it also contained some deviant morphosyntactic features, e.g. copies of Arabic-Persian function words and syntactic patterns, some of which led to considerable sentence complexity. Compounds reflecting Persian noun phrase structure, formed according to the so-called *iżāfet* construction—with a marker connecting adjectival and possessive attributes with their heads—were highly productive in the written language, whereas in spoken Ottoman they only occurred in formulaic expressions. Compound verbs formed according to Persian patterns—based on copied lexical elements with a Turkish auxiliary meaning 'to do' as the second component—were employed in immense numbers. In the more elevated styles, periphrastic verbs of this kind almost totally replaced native Turkish verbs. In nonfinite uses, the Turkish auxiliary could even be omitted.

Other phenomena included Arabic so-called broken plurals, e.g. *meka:tib* 'schools' ← *mekteb*, plural markers such as Arabic {-a:t}, {-i:n}, Persian {-a:n}, even the Arabic dual marker {-eyn}. Gender distinctions, alien to Turkic, were expressed by feminine endings, e.g. *muallime* 'female teacher' ← *muallim*. Adjective attributes could agree in gender with their head in the Arabic way. There were combinational semantic copies such as *gün-be-gün* 'from day to day' (Persian *ru:z-be-ru:z*), with the globally copied Persian preposition *be*.

Ottoman also displayed numerous cases of innovation with respect to the Arabic-Persian-derived material, for instance, the formation of pseudo-Arabic words unknown in Arabic, 'barbarisms', and generally known 'erroneous' expressions, so-called *ɣalata:t-i mešhu:re*. Arabic morphological markers could be added to non-Arabic stems. For example, the noun *ḳira:li:yet* 'kingdom' was formed from the Slavic copied word *ḳira:l* 'king'. Turkish words occasionally occurred with Arabic plural markers to form pseudo-Arabic words, e.g. *gel-iš-a:t* 'circumstances', 'promise of development' ← *gel-iš* 'arrival'. In the last stage of the Ottoman era, many pseudo-Arabic neologisms were coined, mostly designating phenomena of the modern world, e.g. political, scientific, and technological terms.

There are genres of Yiddish, usually limited to religious teaching, that resemble, to some extent, certain genres of Ottoman Turkish in that they incorporate freely not just words but entire phrases from written Hebrew. These are cases of intertwining in the sense that they involve the integration of an entire subsystem into the language. An exceptional example of strong Hebrew influence on a specific Yiddish scribal language is mentioned in Jacobs (2005: 295–296).

7.4 New Persian Take-over Influence on Chaghatay

Chaghatay, another candidate for a subtype of Type 1 (11.2), was the transregional Turkic literary language of Central Asia and other eastern parts of the Turkic-speaking world from the 15th to the early 20th century. Since its path of development was similar to that of Ottoman, it will not be dealt with in detail here. The Chaghatay vocabulary was overloaded with lexemes of Arabic-Persian origin, whereas elements such as pronouns, simple verb stems, etc. were of Turkic origin, e.g. (35).

(36) High-copying Chaghatay
    Ger saŋa   müškil   er-ür   bu iš,   er-ür   a:sa:n
    if   you.DAT difficult be-INTRA3SG this work be-INTRA3SG easy
    maŋa.
    I.DAT
    'If this work is difficult for you, it is easy for me.' (Eckmann 1966: 212).

Of Persian origin: *a:sa:n* 'easy', *(e)ger* 'if', of Arabic origin: *müškil* 'difficult', of Turkic origin: *iš* 'work', *bu* 'this', *saŋa* 'to you' < *sen* 'thou' + DATIVE, *maŋa* 'to me' 'I' + DATIVE, *er-* 'to be' in the simple intraterminal ('present') form *er-ür*. Note that the first occurrence of *er-* in this sentence is not a conditional form *er-se*, which would be expected in normal Turkic syntax.

The designation Chaghatay has its origin in the name of Chinggis Khan's second son, who inherited most Central Asian parts of the Mongol empire in 1227. After the conquests of Timur Lenk (Tamerlan), who came to power in 1405, the language Chaghatay spread as a transregional literary language over the entire Turkic-speaking parts of Central Asia.

Chaghatay, often called Turki, was a Uyghur-Karluk (SE) Turkic language with some Kipchak (NW) Turkic and Oghuz (SW) Turkic elements. Chaghatay continued the traditions from the Karakhanid and Khorezmian literary languages of the East Middle Turkic period. It was the precursor of the modern literary languages Uzbek and Uyghur. However, since the old Uzbeks originally spoke a Kipchak Turkic language, it is incorrect to refer to Chaghatay as 'Old Uzbek', Russian *starouzbekskij jazyk*, which was its official designation in the Soviet Union. Chaghatay texts were written in a vast territory in Islamic Eurasia by speakers of different varieties of Turkic. Its centers of literary activity shifted in time and space, e. g. Kashgar, Surkhandarya, Khwarezm, Samarkand, Herat, Ferghana, and Northern India. A great deal of variation is found in Chaghatay texts. Owing to the complex mingling of Turkic-speaking populations and the shifting geographical centers, it is impossible to establish a specific dialectal basis for Chaghatay. On its linguistic features see Eckmann (1966) and Bodrogligeti (2001).

Classical Chaghatay is the high literary language of the 15th–16th centuries, cultivated in Samarkand, Herat, and other centers of the Timurid realm. Some of the greatest works of Islamic literature, texts belonging to the canon of high-style prose and poetry, were written in this language. The leading Chaghatay poet Mir ᶜAlī Šer Nävā'ī (1441–1501) developed it to a magnificent medium of literary expression, an unrivaled model for subsequent generations of writers. A famous piece of work is the autobiography *Bāburnāme* 'Book of Babur', written by Zahīru'd-dīn Muḥammed Bābur (1483–1530), the Timurid ruler and first Moghul emperor.

Chaghatay was an Islamic language, written in Arabic script and developing under the impact of the Islamic civilization and the increasing orientation towards urban culture. It was originally a lower-ranking written code, characterized by an abundance of Arabic-Persian lexical copies and a complex syntax copied from Persian. The Mongolian influence, however, was restricted to lexical copies from the domains of warfare and administration. The Persan impact was a result of widespread bilingualism. Throughout its entire life cycle, literary Chaghatay coexisted with literary Persian, most of its authors being bilingual in Turkic and Persian. Much of Chaghatay literature consists of translations from Persian. Interestingly enough, Mir ᶜAlī Šēr Nävā'ī argued, in his famous treatise *Muhākamat al-luɣatayn* 'Judgement of the Two Languages', that 'Türkī' was superior, or at least not inferior, to Persian (Devereux 1966).

It should be clear from this short sketch that Chaghatay was a highly developed and, at the same time, flexible written language. It reached the level of a high ranking code, uniting a widespread literate readership. Later Chaghatay became the dominant written language of Central Asia, eventually conquering an immense area of validity and developing regional varieties. It remained the literary language of all non-Oghuz Muslim Turks until a century ago. A premodern period of development, from the 16th century onwards, led to increasing influence of the dialects of the local spoken languages and thus to a number of regional varieties, e.g. in Western Turkistan, Eastern Turkistan (*Kāšyar tili*), the Volga region, the Crimea, and Turkmenistan. This was a preparatory stage preceding the formation of a number of modern written Turkic languages. In Soviet Central Asia, Chaghatay disappeared from use in the 1920s and was replaced by the modern Uzbek standard language.

8   Examples of Type 2: Carry-over Copying

Copies from a lower-ranking code are carried over into a deviant variety of higher-ranking code.

8.1   *Prākrit Carry-over Influence on Deviant Sanskrit*

So-called 'Buddhist Hybrid Sanskrit' is sometimes claimed to be a hybrid form combining elements from Sanskrit and local Middle Indic Prākrit languages, and thus referred to as 'mixed Sanskrit'. It is rather the product of copies of Prākrit linguistic features carried over to non-canonical written versions of Sanskrit. Some authors claim that it would rather merit the designation 'Buddhist Hybrid Prākrit'. For a first attempt to describe its grammar and vocabulary see Edgerton (1953).

Prākrit vernaculars were early used for Buddhist writing in various regions of India and eventually codified. Texts in local languages contributed to the accessibility of Buddhist teaching. What is called 'Buddhist Hybrid Sanskrit' appeared after Sanskrit, owing to Pāṇini's efforts in the 5th century BCE, had begun to become the dominant literary language throughout India. Buddhist scriptures in local Prākrit languages were now translated into versions of the higher-ranking language Sanskrit to grant them greater authority. This led to the emergence of written varieties used almost exclusively for religious texts. Regional variation played an important role. The texts of the northern Buddhist scriptures were mostly composed in such varieties. With the spread of Buddhism outside India, further innovative features were added. 'Buddhist Hybrid Sanskrit' is well-known as the language of the collection *Mahāvastu* 'The great story', dealing with the legendary life of the Buddha and produced by the Mahāsāṅghika school of early Buddhism.

'Buddhist Hybrid Sanskrit' varieties do not represent mainstream Sanskrit. Texts of this tradition have often been mistaken for normal Sanskrit texts, and it has been doubted that the varieties in question are distinct enough from Sanskrit to constitute a separate category. However, the translated texts deviate significantly from the rules of mainstream Sanskrit, displaying innovations copied from local Prākrit varieties in certain domains. They exhibit a specific vocabulary, certain simplified grammatical forms and expressions that are not used by non-Buddhist writers. The deviations are not errors resulting from incomplete knowledge of Pāṇini's system. The varieties in question were written varieties in their own right, not simply Prākrit varieties under heavy Sanskrit impact. 'Buddhist Hybrid Sanskrit' was designed as a specific new 'religiolect', a simplified version of Sanskrit that differed from other varieties. Its creators carried over linguistic habits typical of their local vernaculars into their deviant version of the prestige language Sanskrit.

'Buddhist Hybrid English' (Griffiths 1981) is an analogous, but inadequate, designation suggested for modern translation texts that coin new English phrases and employ English words in semantically anomalous ways, e.g. *own-being* for Sanskrit *svabhāva*, in order to render Buddhist originals in a faithful way.

8.2 *Indic Carry-over Influence on Deviant Written Chinese*

'Buddhist Chinese' was a 'religiolect' created for the dissemination of Buddhist ideas in East Asia (Meisig 2008a). It came into existence during processes of translating Buddhist texts from Sanskrit and Prākrit into Chinese. The translations were interspersed with copied elements, e.g. Indic lexemes and features of Indic word order, to the effect that contemporaneous Chinese readers perceived it as a kind of secret language. 'Buddhist Chinese' is still largely unintelligible to educated Chinese and probably even to most Sinologists.

8.3 Japanese Carry-over Influence on Deviant Written Chinese

So-called Sino-Japanese varieties, which have been characterized as 'mixed', offer several phenomena of interest to our topic.

The study of Chinese in Japan began in the 5th century, motivated by the great prestige of the Chinese culture and the lack of a native writing system for Japanese. In Heian times (794–1192) and beyond, classical Chinese was a prestige language for officials and scholars, much like Latin in the West. It led to take-over copying of Chinese lexical elements into early forms of literary Japanese.

In the further course of Japanese language history, it became a common practice to read texts written with Chinese characters in Japanese wording. For an authoritative survey of the tradition to read Chinese as though it were Japanese see Miller (1967). I am much indebted to my colleagues Tooru Hayasi and Martine Robbeets for valuable supplementary information on the topic.

Kanbun 'Chinese writing' stands for certain types of texts produced from the late Heian period onwards. It does not refer to a language or to language varieties, but to styles of writing. It was originally used for classical Chinese texts written with Chinese characters and read in Chinese wording. The term *junkanbun* refers to classical Chinese literary texts read in Chinese and displaying normal Chinese syntax. The term *kanbun* was, however, also used for the reading of Chinese texts in Japanese wording. Different *kundoku* systems of writing, designating Japanese words with Chinese characters, were used by scholars, priests, and other officials.

Kanbun-kundoku styles stand for various kinds of 'semantic reading' of Chinese texts. The texts were strongly modified. Thus, Japanese function elements were added in *hiragana* script. The Chinese characters were read with Japanese pronunciation according to their meaning-value. *Hentai kanbun* 'deviant Chinese writing', sometimes translated as 'variant Chinese' (Minegishi 1986, Rabinovitch 1996), was widely used throughout the premodern period. It was not a mixed language, but meant reading Chinese texts according to Japanese word order. The pronunciation was *ondoku* 'sound reading', a Sino-Japanese phonological interpretation of the original sound value of the Chinese characters. This manner of rendering Chinese texts, something never used in natural spoken language, was, as Miller puts it, 'a kind of lazy schoolboy's trot to a classical text' (1967: 31).

Japanese scholars and officials developed a specific written version of Chinese, into which Japanese elements were carried over and which thus deviated from the norms of standard Chinese. It was a method for reading Chinese; texts written according to it were composed in order to be read out in Japanese. An important device was *kunten*, an annotation technique for reading and deciphering Chinese texts. The method of reading Chinese according to this system evolved gradually, growing more complex and systematized. It became the normal way of reading Chinese texts and functioned as a form of Japanese in its own right.

The effect of practicing this method was that Chinese and Japanese were virtually treated as if they were the same language. Writers were often not really aware of which language they were writing in. Miller writes: "If a Chinese text when read and studied sounded just like a Japanese text, it was indeed and for all practical purposes a Japanese text. And if you wrote Chinese and read Japanese, why not go one step further and write Chinese even when the intention from the beginning was to read /.../ Japanese" (1967: 131).

Among the codes used in the literate society of the Heian period, written Japanese enjoyed much less prestige than this kind of deviant Chinese. This fact reflects the close ties to China and the wish to emulate the advanced culture transmitted by means of the Chinese language. The direct Chinese influence on Japanese was highly limited, since utterly few native speakers of Chinese lived in Japan.

'Variant Chinese' eventually evolved as a distinct Japanese literary style. It was the preferred choice for official materials, used in court records, government documents, formal correspondence and private journals and memoirs kept by emperors, the civil nobility, military leaders, and scholars. It was also employed in literary or quasi-literary genres, e.g. historical narratives. Certain forms of 'variant Chinese' displayed relatively few deviations from orthodox Chinese grammar and relatively few Japanese lexemes. Others exhibited higher degrees of deviation from Chinese norms. This *kiroku-tai* 'documentary form' became increasingly more Japanese-like in vocabulary and syntax and was thus not intelligible to readers without a knowledge of Japanese. It was characterized by features that native Chinese speakers would consider ungrammatical. Fewer *kundoku* markings were eventually needed, and less syntactic rearrangement was required in order for a text to be read as Japanese. Japanese glosses were generally not attached to common words of Chinese origin.

The grammar was simplified as compared to Chinese written in China. Japanese syntactic structures gave rise to deviations from Chinese norms. Rabinovitch cites some examples of characteristic features (1996: 121–126). Common phenomena included reversal of verb and object, OV order instead of VO, reversal of subject and predicate, and separation of modifying phrases from the modified head. Rabinovitch mentions misplacement of Japanese 'auxiliary verb suffixes'. The auxiliaries in question were obviously particles rather than suffixes, e.g. honorific elements such as Japanese {-raru}. The auxiliary *beki* 'should', 'ought to' could occur after the main verb, contrary to conventional Chinese syntax. Japanese honorific forms were introduced. The use of Japanese vocabulary was virtually unrestricted. Chinese-like neologisms were coined, e.g. *jikkon ~ jukkon* 'friendly', 'intimate'. Lexical copies from Chinese were semantically adapted, assuming meanings that diverged from classical Chinese usage.

The orthographic features included the use of Chinese *kanji* logographs intermingled with Japanese *kana* syllabographs and other characters unknown in China. The modern Japanese writing system still uses *kanji* and *kana* side by side. Chinese logographs were also used for neologisms created in Japan. They were thus read in a complex way, not only with Chinese-like values, but also with Japanese values.

Rabinovitch mentions the use of rebus orthographies based on purely phonetic coincidences between words, e.g. *mutsukashi* 'difficult', a combination of *mutsu* 'six' and *kashi* 'to lend', which are homophonous but semantically unrelated (1996: 125).

According to the analysis presented above, 'variant Chinese' represents Type B. Users of the lower-ranking code Japanese carried over copies of elements from this code to their deviant variety of the higher-ranking written code Chinese. As in similar cases, it is doubtful whether these styles of written Japanese really originated in imperfect attempts to write Chinese.

'Variant Chinese' later developed to a distinct Japanese literary style, coexisting and interacting with written Japanese and Chinese in complex ways, in a continuous cycle of copying processes. One variety was *kanbun-kundoku-tai*, a Japanese code characterized by strong take-over influence from Chinese. It contained numerous copies of Chinese lexemes, whereas the system morphemes were mainly Japanese. Certain indigenous Japanese lexemes were exclusively used in this variety. On the other hand, elements of 'variant Chinese' were eventually copied into literary Japanese, which thus acquired structures that were originally alien to it. Many modern constructions go back to the old intertwined styles.

8.4 *Mongolian Carry-over Influence on Deviant Written Chinese*

During the Mongol (Yüan) rule in China, partially from 1215, entirely 1279–1368, a written variety emerged that has been called Hybrid Chinese or Mongolized Chinese (Zograf 1989, de Rachewiltz 1996). This deviant Chinese variety developed as a result of heavy carry-over influence from Mongolian. It was used in what is called 'Yüan officialese', a formal style characteristic of official documents issued by government and local administration bureaus. The documents were verbatim translations of Mongolian texts, closely corresponding to the originals. The translators carried over copies from Mongolian into their own vernacular-oriented variety of Chinese. Characteristic features include copies of Mongolian vocabulary, morphology, and syntax, as well as combinational semantic copies of Mongolian chancellery formulae.

Mongolian influence is also found in translations of Chinese classics into a similar vernacular-based written language. Popular plays of the Yüan and even the Ming period contain lexical and grammatical Mongolisms, rendered in Chinese phonetic transcription. Mongolian words frequently occur in mixed Chinese-Mongolian scenes, which mirror the spoken language, for example, (*h*)*ala* 'kill!', *anda* 'sworn friend', *ba:tur* 'hero', 'brave', *darasun* 'wine', *ma'u* 'bad', *miqan* 'meat', *morin* 'horse', *numu*(*n*) 'bow', *qulaqai* 'thief', *sadun* 'relative', *sauqa* 'gift', *sayin* 'good', *tana* 'large pearl', 'jewel', *teri'ün* 'head', 'chief', *ula'ači* 'groom', *ügei* 'not', 'nothing' (Waley 1957).

The grammatical peculiarities of this 'hybrid Chinese' are also found in the translation of Chinese classics into the vernacular. Texts by Kuan Yün-Shih (1286–1324) thus exhibit an 'unmistakenly hybrid Chinese-Mongol flavour' (de Rachewiltz 1996: 906). There is, for instance, an element that corresponds to the Mongolian copula *bui*, *buyu* 'is', 'are', etc. and serves as an affirmative final particle. Both this text type and 'Yüan officialese' display syntactic copies such as the use of Mongolian *ke'en* or *ke'ejü* 'saying' to indicate quotations.

8.5 *Manchu Carry-over Influence on Deviant Written Chinese*

So-called *zidi shu* texts, sometimes referred to as 'mixed Chinese-Manchu texts', document how Manchu speakers in China carried over copies from their primary code to their own variety of Chinese. The Manchus conquered China in 1644 and established the Qing dynasty, which lasted until 1911. Manchu became the first language at the imperial court. For two centuries it was the main language of government and served as a lingua franca. Literary works of the Qing period were, however, written in Chinese. By the middle of the 19th century, numerous Manchus had shifted to Chinese as their first language and lost fluency in their native language. Nonetheless, imperial documents were produced in both Manchu and Chinese until the end of the Qing dynasty.

Manchu is a Tungusic language of Northeast China with utterly few native speakers left today. It is very close to the Shibe language, spoken near the Ili valley in Xinjiang by descendants of a group that was moved there in 1764. Written Manchu exhibited a high degree of regularity and simplicity, thus differing considerably from the spoken languages of the Tungusic family. It possessed a large amount of Chinese and Mongolian lexical copies and also some nonnative phonological features copied from Chinese. On written Manchu see Haenisch (1961) and Gorelova (2002).

The *zidi shu* texts represent a special genre that emerged under the Qing dynasty: lyrical texts or songs composed in an unusual linguistic style. They belong to a type of performance art called *quyi* and were initiated by the *baqi* 'the Eight Banners', Manchu *gûsa*, the basic administrative framework of the Manchu military organization. The texts are highly important for the study of contacts between Chinese and Manchu. They are indicative of the linguistic situation in Northern China in the Qing period, probably mirroring the typical language of the numerous Manchu bannermen who lived in and around Beijing. It is, however, unknown whether the texts represent a common form of songs of their period and what kind of audience they were performed for (Wadley 1991: 5).

Okada (1992) dealt with *zidi shu* texts as products of Chinese-Manchu language contacts and published facsimiles of two of them. *Katuri jetere zidi shu* and *Cha guan zidi shu* were edited by Wadley (1991). Wadley also undertook to analyze the language of the texts in a framework of contact-induced change, drawing attention to the existence of numerous copies of Manchu lexical items as well as influences in phonology and, especially, in the domain of syntax, e.g. occasional SOV constituent order. His conclusion is that these features are results of imperfect learning during a process of language shift to Chinese, i.e. errors made by members of the shifting group. The texts may document one developmental stage on the road to the extinction of the Manchu language. The texts may certainly mirror the shift of a group of Manchu speakers to Chinese, but they do not prove that the authors had failed to learn standard Chinese. It is equally conceivable that they had developed their own variety of Chinese, to which they carried over copies from their primary Manchu code.

Interestingly enough, this deviant variety seems to have exerted considerable influence on Chinese as spoken in the Beijing region. The features appear to have been imitated by original speakers of Chinese and spread to other varieties. This contradicts the widespread assumption that Chinese is essentially resistant to outside influence. The overwhelming cultural dominance of the Chinese civilization in pre-20th-century Asia has been thought to preclude the possibility of any external influence on Chinese. Thus, Li & Thompson supposed that any change observed in Chinese word order must have originated 'internally' (1974: 206). This view of Chinese as a closed system has been challenged recently. The study of areal linguistic features, especially in northern China, may provide valuable new information on the development of Chinese. The late Hashimoto Mantarō, who took a particular interest in *zidi shu* texts, advocated this in a number of contributions (Wadley 1996).

9 Examples of Type 3: Alternate Use of the Codes

Type 3 covers cases in which segments of a given text are composed in two different languages. The text contains elements of a lower-ranking code that alternate with elements of a higher-ranking code. Such products of textual mixture have sometimes been characterized as written in mixed languages. Some examples will be given below.

Alternation is typical of bilingual cultures, especially of diglossic situations. The linguistic situation holding in the bilingual community is reflected in a specific choice of languages. The functions of the languages are mostly distinguished, each being used in particular situations or for particular purposes. In the literature, bilingual writing of this kind often has specific artistic functions. It may be used for humorous, travestying purposes, or, in more serious texts, as an aesthetic device, e.g. for lyrical effects in bilingual poems.

9.1 Mixed Poems

Type 3 is represented by medieval poetic texts showing alternation between Latin and a European vernacular. European bilingual poetry goes back at least to the Middle Ages, to a period when Latin was still the language of intellectuals, though it began to lose ground to the vernaculars. Numerous medieval European poems are written in a mixture of Latin and a vernacular. *Carmina Burana*, collected around 1230, contain poems in which Latin alternates with Medieval German or French. The text of the Christmas carol *In dulci jubilo*, written by Heinrich Seuse (c. 1300–1366), alternates Latin with German, e.g. *In dulci jubilo, nun singet und seid froh* 'In sweet rejoicing, now sing and be glad'. On mixed sermons in Medieval England see Wenzel (1994).

Genuine macaronic texs are of a somewhat different nature (Perini 2001). The word *macaronicus* emerged in the late 14th century from dialectal Italian *maccarone* 'macaroni', a kind of pasta eaten by peasants. The oldest example is thought to be Tifi Odasi's comical poem *Macaronea* of the 15th century (Paoli 1959, Paccagnella 1979). Macaronic texts are the product of a scholarly exercise, composed to ridicule the broken Latin written in certain learned circles. The texts often contain vernacular words or 'Latinized' Italian words provided with Latin endings. For instance, when Tibi Odasi writes *facit tremare pilastros* 'makes the pillars tremble', he uses *tremare* instead of Latin *tremere*, a syntactic calque on the model of vulgar *far tremare*, and a masculine plural *pilastros*, instead of a neutral plural that would be expected if *pilastro* were 'Latinized' as *pilastrum*.

Francesco Colonna's *Hypnerotomachia Poliphili* (1499) used Italian syntax and morphology, but a vocabulary made up of Latin and Greek elements.

Humorous texts of this kind became highly popular in the 16th and 17th centuries.

The *muwaššaha* of Muslim Spain were mostly written in Arabic and contained a coda with archaic Spanish elements. For example, the poet would express, in the higher-ranking language Arabic, his love to a slave girl, whereupon the girl replied in the lower-ranking language of the people (Forster 1970: 12).

In the traditional Oriental world, mixed poems of this kind were known as *mulamma*, sometimes called 'patch-work poems' or 'pied verse' (Browne 1906: 66). For example, they were common under the Muslim rule in medieval India. Poems were written alternatingly in two languages, with Hindi verses followed by Persian verses or vice versa. A master of this style was the Sufi poet Amīr Khusrow Dehlawī (1253–1325 CE). Many other examples could be added. In early Armeno-Turkic literature, for instance, Armenian poems were intercalated by Turkic verses (Berberian 1964: 813–814).

The kind of intertwining we are concerned with here is thus code alternation in written texts. It is not a matter of inserting elements of one code into a text written in another code. Neither of the codes can be considered the Basic Code of the whole text. One of them is basic in certain portions, the other one in other portions. There may be a more or less regular alternation from stanza to stanza, from line to line, or from half-line to half-line.

A text of this kind addresses an audience that is sufficiently bilingual to understand and appreciate it. Even if the whole poem is of popular nature, it presupposes knowledge of more than one of the languages involved. Its complex functions make it less translatable than monolingual texts. It must be rendered in as many codes as it was composed in, and the specific functions of these codes must be somehow reproduced. In certain situations, polyphonic texts of this kind may express a wish for seclusion. A specific mixture may thus be used to exclude monolingual groups as addressees. Foreign elements in poetry, however, do not always presuppose a polyglot audience. In particular cases of stylistic use, the understanding of the foreign elements may not be essential or not even intended (Elwert 1972).

In European medieval literature as well as in traditional Oriental literature, the language choice was basically determined by the genre and not by the author's nationality. Language alternation varied from literature to literature, and, within the same culture, from period to period, according to the tolerance of the audience, the literary genre, the taste of the period, and the stylistic intentions of the author (Elwert 1960, 1972). The technique can be reduced to a few basic types, but each type is rather variable.

Alternation may originate in very different motives and serve various aesthetic effects. The use of foreign elements in poetry is essentially a stylistic problem with a broad diversity of motivations. The question of how the two codes used are interrelated is intricate, especially since too little is known in general about the organization of languages coexisting in the same mind. As a rule, it is not possible to switch freely between the languages. They serve different purposes, with unique functions that cannot be fulfilled by the other component. One language may characterize a milieu, supplying local color or demonstrating artistic virtuosity. Certain kinds of intercalations may serve humorous purposes. Bilingual poems are often produced when a language of a high emotional value is used together with a culturally dominant one, a higher-ranking code. The use of a much liked language that is otherwise not employed for literary purposes may convey a pleasant flavour to a poem.

Biliteracy as poetic technique is attested in many literary genres in the Middle Ages. For Latin in German poems see Grünewald (1908), Henrici (1913); for Latin in French poems see Müller (1919). The higher-ranking code is in general an established literary medium and can as such serve, as it were, as a kind of tutor or mentor to the lower-ranking code. It is easier to write in a language that offers rich stylistic facilities than to transfer these facilities into an 'unpracticed' language.

Up to the Romantics, European poets often wrote Latin with greater ease than their mother tongue. They preferred Latin, since it offered them familiar models of poetic diction, a prefabricated system of expressions and formulae, patterns of wording and versification. Poets would form their style in the less elaborated language and learned to master its stylistic resources by reformulating what they had already formulated in the dominant literary language. European poets would translate their own Latin poems as an exercise to develop their diction in the vernacular. European Renaissance poets often wrote in their mother tongue as if it were Latin, profiting from an established style ready for use. Reformulation of formulae acquired in a second language, *imitatio*, was, however, not always an easy task. Many authors writing brilliant Latin poems were relatively helpless when trying to master their vernacular (Forster 1970: 33).

Bilingual poems can help activate a literarily non-active popular language, even if the poems are not written with this aim. The mixed structure allows the poet to exercise the literarily non-elaborated language in the framework of a poem in the elaborated language. The poem is not only a model, but it constitutes the structural framework itself.

The situation was similar in the Orient. Mir ᶜAli-Šer Nävā'ī, the first major Turkic poet to use his Turkic vernacular, testifies, in his above-mentioned treatise *Muhākamat al-luyatayn* (1499), that it is easier for the beginner to write in Persian: The novice gets annoyed with the difficulties connected with composing poetry in Turkic and inclines to the 'easier' language, in this case Persian. When poets of Khorasan and Transoxiana first tried to write Turkic poems in the Arabic-Persian ʿarūz meter, they probably started with Turkic-Persian *mulamma* verses (Köprülü 1964: 253). Also in the Azeri area with its Persian dominance, poets early began to write *mulamma* in Persian and the Turkic vernacular (Caferoğlu 1964).

The situation found here is thus often the beginning of the use of a lower-ranking code for literary purposes. It may be a preliminary stage of literature written in the dominated language, a first sign of the emergence of a new literary medium. Periods of bi- or multilingualism have been decisive for the emergence of many literary languages. Mixed verses may mark the multilingual starting-point of a literary development. The bilingual texts are exponents of a certain stage in the typical 'Ausbau' process of new language varieties on their way to performing more qualified communicative tasks (Kloss 1952). The language is, typically, first practiced for humorous or folkloristic purposes, then adopted by lyric writers, and finally used by prose narrators.

The mixed poetry of Amīr Khusrow Dehlawī played a major role for the emergence of Urdu as a written language. Written Persian played a substantial role for the beginnings of a Turkic high literature. It offered a developed vocabulary, poetic models, pre-existing styles, and a ready-made diction. The Anatolian Seljuk court culture, including the literary education, was basically Persian. Turkish, which was considered *kaba* 'rough', did not yet serve as a literary medium, a poetic tool which poets could have used immediately and adequately for their purposes. The Anatolian cultural center Konya was the multilingual environment in which the great poet Jelāleddīn Rūmī (1207–1273) created his Sufic chefs-d'œuvre in a highly elaborated Persian style.

In addition, he also wrote a few simple Turkic verses, mostly Persian-Turkic *mulammaʿāt*, playful mixtures of segments in two languages. The Turkic component, which contains an everyday vocabulary, stands for modest, intimate elements of everyday life, referring to the private life of the poet. I have suggested that these poems are closely connected with the birth of Turkish poetry (Johanson 1993a). They are less likely to fulfill, as has been claimed, subversive functions. In Rūmī's *mulamma* verses, the texts sometimes show a very close integration of the two languages: a sentence may consist of phrases from both. In one poem, almost every half-line ends in a Turkish sequence, e.g. *zān-i šakar labānat* 'from those sweet lips of yours' (Persian) *Bir öpkinen diler men* (Turkish) 'I want a little kiss'. In some other cases, the Turkish element just consists of direct quotations.

9.2 Bilingual Hebrew-Romance Texts

Hebrew-Romance varieties based on Romance dialects were, in the Middle Ages, spoken by Jewish communities e.g. in Spain, Catalonia, and Provence, where they acquired a certain recognition as languages in their own right. Bilingual Hebrew-Romance texts written in Hebrew script were produced in many diaspora communities. Regional Romance varieties were, to various degrees, used to compose texts serving liturgical purposes or employed at other ceremonies and celebrations: hymns, prayers, elegies, songs, poems, etc. Though they represent various categories of bilingual poetic practice, their common feature is alternation of verses in the two languages, sometimes with the Romance and Hebrew verses rhyming with each other.

Some texts are the works of known Jewish poets in Provence, Spain, and Italy. Interesting examples of bilingual texts are found in Lazar (1971), an edition of four songs, *épthalamia*, that are documented in 15th century manuscripts and were probably composed in the 14th century. It contains three Provençal-Catalan songs and a fourth one, which was composed in Spain, but probably copied in Italy, since it reflects the Aragon dialect with Italianisms. For the use of Hebrew in French poems see Blondheim (1926a, 1926b).

9.3 Manchu-Chinese Mixed Poetry

Manchu-Chinese mixed poems known as *manju nikan yangsanggai acamjiha ucun* represent a similar type, and should not be confused with the deviant Chinese texts referred to as *zidi shu* mentioned above. This genre is regarded as artistic poetry at a high level, reminiscent of T'ang poetry and composed according to very rigid principles of the simultaneous use of the two languages (Stary 1985: 203).

9.4 Mixed Text Types in Medieval British Writing

Medieval England was characterized by multiliteracy. The three languages Middle English, Anglo-Norman, and Medieval Latin interacted systematically in certain text types of late medieval British writing (Schendl 1996, 1997). Many legal texts were trilingual, but the three languages occurred in discrete monolingual passages. There are comparable later cases, e.g. the relatively long-lived convention in the Channel islands of Guernsey and Jersey, where formal and ceremonial functions, e.g. legal proceedings, required the use of standard French, for which an English translation had to be supplied (Price 2000: 191).

What interests us here is, however, the occurrence of non-monolingual text types. One case in point is the role of Latin-English texts as a medium of administration. A relevant text type used for professional purposes is that of trade:

mixed-language business writing, found in large numbers of documents. Here we are confronted with instances of mixed texts, and not with mixed languages.

The business writing system used from the time of the Norman conquest until the rise of standard English has been discussed by Wright in numerous contributions (e.g. 1995, 1998, 2001a, 2001b, 2002a, 2002b, 2005). Her investigations focus on the language of merchants, particularly of London merchants trading with merchants from abroad.

Medieval business writing in London was not monolingual. Traders and accounts-keepers did not write in their own Middle English dialect, but in a mixture of Middle English and Medieval Latin or Anglo-Norman. The languages were not randomly distributed, but incorporated into the texts in an orderly way. Scribes obviously maintained control over which components belonged to which language. In monolingual Middle English and monolingual Latin text types, the different languages were kept separate, but different principles were applied to bilingual texts. Business writing displayed an orderly mix of Medieval Latin and Middle English. Uniformity was not an ideal strived for in this text type, a useful type that facilitated trading with merchants who spoke and read languages other than English. It even functioned in cases where the English-speaking readers had only a very small grasp of Latin. A text could be read, at least partially, as Medieval Latin or as Middle English. Traders could extract from the texts whatever they needed to know. Two examples of mixed-language business writing in Medieval Latin and English; accounts-keeping for the financial year 1460–1461 (Wright 2000a, 2001b).

(37) Medieval bilingual text
 a. *Reman j vile & j Serra*
  'There remains 1 file and 1 saw.'

 b. *It P j noua serra empt*
  'And for 1 new saw bought.'

 c. *It P j vyle P acuacoe de ley Tide sawes empt & reman xijd*
  'And for 1 file for sharpening of the tidesaws bought and remaining, 12d.'

It was the usual practice in this text type to translate a simplex element such as *saw* into Medieval Latin, *serra*, but to write the word in English if it occurred as part of a compound, *tidesaw*. The scribe knew how to write the word in monolingual Medieval Latin, but used both languages because that was the custom of the text type.

The mixed-language business text type was used all over Britain. Unlike monolingual Middle English texts, which varied greatly from region to region, it was, in its fundamental structure, comparatively stable geographically. Still it is characterized by a range of options. It used a highly developed, sophisticated writing system with variable spelling and heavy use of the medieval abbreviation and suspension system, which enabled writers to exploit overlaps between the languages. Non-standardized spellings and shapes of single lexemes served pragmatic purposes, often suggesting the French or Latin equivalents of the English forms, which was of advantage to traders from different language backgrounds.

In this text type, Middle English was variably used for content words, i.e. nouns, adjectives, and verb stems. Medieval Latin was compulsorily used for function words and variably used for other parts of speech. Both Germanic and Romance word-order and gender agreement rules were applied. As for calques, Middle English patterns were mostly followed for compounds, and Medieval Latin or Anglo-Norman patterns for simplex forms.

The medieval mixed-language text type was in use until the end of the 15th century. It vanished concurrently with processes of standardization owing to changing trade and business patterns. The styles of written English that eventually emerged were decreasingly tolerant of the variation found in this business text type.

10 Examples of Type 4: Lower-Ranking Code Explicates Higher-Ranking Code

In Type 4, a lower-ranking code is used to explicate texts in a higher-ranking code.

10.1 *Japanese Reading Aids for Chinese Texts*

The Japanese *kunten* method mentioned above was an annotation technique for reading and deciphering Chinese texts. It contained reading aids added to allow original texts to be read in Japanese. It rearranged the sentences according to Japanese syntax, provided Japanese glosses for lexemes and added the necessary grammatical elements. The reading aids were written with Japanese syllabograms, dots, and other reading marks.

According to Numamoto (2008), the earliest *kunten* texts were produced in the early Heian period, i.e. in the late 8th century. The *kunten* systems developed under the strong influence of the development of contemporary philological studies by Chinese scholars.

Similar annotation techniques for deciphering Chinese texts are found in Korea, where the annotations were not written with ink, but with a hard thin stick which left a series of dents. This tradition is also known in Japan.

10.2 Burmese Reading Aids for Pali Texts

An interesting similar method, which has erroneously been referred to as a mixed language, is the so-called 'Nissaya Burmese', known from the 15th century onwards. Up to this period, the Sino-Tibetan language Burmese is only known from stone inscriptions. The earliest record is found in the quadrilingual Myazedi inscription (1112), in which one and the same story is told in the four languages Pali, Pyu, Mon, and Burmese.

Pali, an Indo-European, Middle Indic language, unrelated to Burmese, later came to exert a substantial impact on the Burmese history of writing, namely as the language of Theravāda Buddhism. The decisive source was the Pali canon of Buddhism. When Theravāda Buddhism was adopted as the state religion, numerous Pali texts were brought from Ceylon. In spite of translations, Pali remained the main literary medium for centuries. It was one of the various Prākrit languages associated with different religious communities and standing in a specific opposition to Sanskrit, the classical high language of ancient India. Its functions are comparable to 'Buddhist Hybrid Sanskrit' discussed above.

The oldest and most widely known version of the *Tripitaka* 'The three baskets', the canon of the holy scriptures of Buddhism, is the Pali canon, *tipiṭaka*, of the Theravāda school. On Pali and its tradition in Burma see von Hinüber (1978, 1983), Okell (1965, 1967), and Pruitt (1994).

Pali became the high-ranking prestige language of books and learning in Burma. It was held in high esteem and exerted a strong influence on Burmese. A number of copied words from Pali had entered Burmese already at the time of the earliest records. With the introduction of Theravāda Buddhism, some early Sanskrit copied words were replaced by Pali equivalents.

The study of Pali texts flourished in Burma. The Buddhist scriptures were first rendered in Pali with Burmese interlinear translations. This led to the so-called *nissaya* form, in which each Pali word or phrase was followed by its Burmese translation including grammatical markers corresponding to the Pali markers. This procedure is similar to the interlinear glossing practiced in modern linguistic literature. Nissaya texts have been known since at least the mid-15th century, before the emergence of corresponding texts in Burmese. They represent a strong system with widespread acceptance up to modern time. The same grammatical conventions have been preserved for more than four centuries.

This technique was intended to give readers the meaning of the Pali text and to enable them to interpret its grammar. Pali inflections and syntax were represented in an accurate way. The word-by-word arrangement simulated a close structural correspondence with Pali. Burmese is largely monosyllabic, expressing grammatical relations by means of postposed particles. The technique took advantage of the fact that the position of the particles at the end of words made them similar to suffixes. Certain particles were conventionally used to represent number, case, tense, mood, etc. For the student, texts of this kind 'could be a kind of grammar or manual as well as a dictionary' (Okell 1965: 187). By scanning the lines and learning the meaning of Pali words or phrases, the student could also grasp unfamiliar syntactic constructions, e.g. relative clauses, which were rendered according to Pali word order.

Texts of this kind thus served as reading aids, as tools for didactic purposes. They were texts in a foreign higher-ranking code with added information, which aimed at helping to read and understand it. A code of one type was systematically interpreted and reflected in terms of a code of a different type. It would be wrong to claim that Burmese was adapted to represent the structure of Pali, that it was analyzed in terms of Pali structure, or that Pali was relexified in the sense that its lexicon was replaced with Burmese lexical items. The texts were not composed in a mixed language, but represent a different kind of intertwining: a method for reading a higher-ranking code according to the familiar structure of a lower-ranking code. The parallels with the Japanese *hentai kanbun* 'deviant Chinese writing' are obvious. The technique is also reminiscent of Persian and Turkic interlinear Koran translations. The technique is a kind of carry-over influence on a version of a higher-ranking code, even if this version is not necessarily deviant. Interestingly enough, the design of the texts was later modified. Burmese words could be omitted in cases where the Pali words were intelligible. Grammatical markers could also be omitted. Texts could be composed directly in the *nissaya* style without citing a Pali original. The result was written Burmese structured according to *nissaya* conventions. For several centuries, *nissaya* conventions dominated non-*nissaya* Burmese prose, which largely consisted of translations and adaptations of Pali texts. They constituted the basic structure of the written registers, making the texts look as though they were composed in a Pali frame. Burmese sentences were shaped in the same way as their Pali analogs.

Okell (1965) presents 'Nissaya Burmese' as an example of a language of one type that is deliberately and systematically adapted to the structure of a language of another type. His careful analysis of some texts is too detailed to be dealt with in the present survey (1965: 195–226). It may be mentioned that Pali passive constructions are turned into active constructions, since no satisfactory passive construction can be produced in Burmese. Relative clauses receive no special treatment as a whole; each word is rendered just as it stands in the Pali clause. Pali numeral adjectives need special treatment because counting in Burmese entails the use of classifiers. Pronouns are declined in the same way as nouns.

Up to the 20th century, writers modeled their prose on Pali patterns. Burmese grammars were virtually modified Pali grammars in Burmese dress. Owing to stylistic habits, comparable to bookish scribal traditionalism in the treatment of texts in antique languages, plain Burmese prose styles conserved certain *nissaya*-like properties. Some features of Pali grammar were even copied into spoken Burmese. Two separate sets of rules may be necessary to describe the contemporary situation: one set for the more indigenous component, and one set for the Pali-derived component. This segregation would be reminiscent of the compartmentalization observed in written High Ottoman.

10.3 Sinhalese Reading Aids for Pali Texts

Buddhist texts originating from the Indic Sanskrit tradition and translated into Pali were also studied and developed by Sinhalese Buddhists. Their way of handling with Pali texts played a similar role as in the Burmese example. On the Sinhalese Buddhist literature see Bechert (2005); cf. Meisig (2008b). The cultural languages used by the Sinhalese have been literary Sinhala, also called Elu in its more ancient variant, and Pali. The development of literary Sinhala is characterized by lexical copying from Sanskrit and Neo-Sanskrit and, to a high degree, by Pali influence. Literary Sinhala differs considerably from colloquial Sinhala.

10.4 Karaim Reading Aids for Hebrew Texts

A similar language of translation is found in what the Turkic-speaking Karaims called *peshaṭ*, a piece of literal exegesis that pursued the 'plain sense' of Old Testament texts, a word-by-word translation of Hebrew originals. This was the way Karaim scholars, educated in Biblical Hebrew, translated texts into their Kipchak Turkic vernacular. The oldest known translation in Southwest Karaim is from the 16th century and the oldest one in Northwest Karaim is from the 18th century. The translations were meant to make the Hebrew original understandable and also to show its linguistic structure. This way of translating became a kind of biblical exegesis. In order to mirror the original structure of the text, the translators copied various linguistic features of the Hebrew original. The resulting texts bear evidence of strong adherence to the Hebrew origin and are characterized by non-Turkic syntactic features.

The syntax shows, like the Hebrew original, the word order noun + genitive, i.e. the possessor often follows the head noun, e.g. *alyiš-ï Tenri-nin* ⟨blessing-POSS3SG God-GEN⟩ 'God's blessing' instead of *Tenri-nin alyiš-ï*. The order noun + adjective tends to be the same as in the Hebrew original, contrary to the normal Turkic word order. The demonstrative pronoun *ol* 'she/he/it' functions, against the general rule in Turkic languages, as an article that corresponds systematically to the Hebrew definite article *ha*. The enclitic *da* 'and', which is postpositive in other Turkic languages, is preposed on the model of Hebrew {wa-}.

The following example shows a part of an original Hebrew sentence from the book of Genesis and its Northwest Karaim *peshaṯ* translation (Olach 2013).

(38) Hebrew Bible text
    a. Hebrew original
        wərū^aḥ   *'ēlōhîm*
        and wind of.CONJ.N:BOTH.SG.CONST God
        mərahépeṯ   *'al-*
        hovering.V:PIEL.PTCP.FEM.SG.ABS over.PREP
        pəné   *hammáyim.*
        faces of.N:BOTH.PL.CONST the waters.DEF.N:MASC.PL.ABS
        'and the spirit of God was moving over the face of the waters'

    b. Northwest Karaim translation
        da   yel-i   *t'en'r'in'in' t'öbr'än'ir ed'i*
        and wind-POSS3SG God-GEN stir.up AOR COP-PAST3SG
        yüz'-l'är'i   üs't'-ün'-ä   ol suv-lar-niŋ
        face-POSS3PL surface-POSS3-DAT the water-PL-GEN
        'and the wind of God was blowing on the face of the waters' (Olach 2013:83)

It is a matter of controversy to what extent the Karaim language, in particular spoken Karaim, has been influenced by biblical Hebrew through these literal translations. The habit to translate Biblical texts word by word in a 'slavish' way is sometimes thought to have been most important reason for the syntactic changes in Karaim. The language would have developed under strong continuous influence of the sacral language Hebrew, and the *peshaṯ* translation tradition would have caused far-reaching changes. Shapira argues that the learned language of translation "was unnatural, copying Hebrew modes and syntax, but enjoyed a high status" (2003: 668).

Turcologists have acknowledged the influence of Hebrew on the language of the translations, without ascribing the non-Turkic properties of Karaim solely to copying from Hebrew. Typological changes in Karaim have also been induced by the long-lasting influence of Slavic and Baltic languages known to the Karaims, e.g. Polish, Russian, White Russian, Ruthenian, and, more recently, Lithuanian. The Slavic influence is strongest in the colloquial language and manifests itself in a large number of copied words and idiomatic expressions translated literally from Slavic (Kowalski 1929: xxxviii–xxxix). Hebrew has not necessarily played a decisive role in the formation of Karaim (Musaev 1964: 32).

Csató (2000) argues that the word order properties of Karaim developed under the influence of the non-Turkic contact languages of the area. Karaim biblical translations show pecularities which can be explained as a result of the one-to-one mapping of the structure of the Hebrew original. However, the word order properties of the spoken language cannot be traced back solely to the influence of those translations. They are results of changes induced by contact with the non-Turkic languages of the area in which the Karaim speakers live. Several typological features have been acquired through intensive copying from non-Turkic languages: the basic VO order, the noun + genitive order, and the use of relative clauses introduced by a relativizer. The typological coincidence between areal features and certain properties of biblical Hebrew reinforced each other. But Karaim did not acquire features that are found only in the Bible translations. It does not use *ol* as a definite article. It did not copy the Hebrew noun + adjective order, which is not typical of the Circum-Baltic area.

11 Examples of Type 5: Higher-Ranking Code Represents Lower-Ranking Code

Type 5 implies that a message in a lower-ranking code is represented by writing in a higher-ranking code. Written records do not necessarily render the original wording of a message. A text composed in one code may be dealt with as though it were a text in another code.

'Alloglottography', a term coined by Gershevitch (1979), is the technique of representing an utterance in one language by using the writing system of another language. It means writing a text in a code different from the code in which it is intended to be read, i.e. one code is used for writing a text and another code for reading it. This technique manifests a loyalty to a high-ranking code and its script regardless of the acts of reading. It is commonly used in situations of restricted literacy, when a language does not have a writing system of its own.

The higher-ranking codes used for writing—prestige languages, often ritual languages or politically dominant languages of forceful states—offer cultivated formal ways of expression. Cross-culturally, alloglottography is not an unusual phenomenon. It was common in the Ancient Near East, at least partially in cuneiform writing. It was later widely used in many regions, e.g. in the Caucasus region before the spread of Christianity. Prior to the introduction of the alphabetic system, Georgian was represented by means of the Aramaic writing system. The old *man'yōgana* system represented Japanese in Chinese writing with Chinese characters used as logograms and phonetic syllable symbols. In Medieval Europe, sermons were often written in Latin, but intended to be delivered in the vernaculars. Alloglottography requires special skills and was traditionally handled by specialized scribes mastering *extempore* translation techniques. Remnants of these old traditions still exist in the Middle East. A scribe in Iran may, for example, produce a document in Persian, though the customer dictates it in Azeri.

11.1 Semitic Represented in Sumerian Writing

The representation of Semitic languages in Sumerian writing is the first known example of alloglottography. The oldest known writing system was invented in Mesopotamia in the 3rd millennium BCE. In the proto-literate period, it was a pictographic system, a script based on pictorial representations of objects. The system developed into a cuneiform script, which was first used for Sumerian. It was based on pictograms, but it also used other devices which changed it into a script system. The scribes took advantage of the homophony of certain words that differed in meaning. For instance, they would draw the sign for 'reed' also in order to express 'to return', since the two words had the same pronunciation, namely *gi*. At this stage, the signs thus denoted words and not objects.

The principle of phonetic similarity was further developed. A sound script was invented. Signs standing for syllables could be added to words. Many signs could stand for both a word and a syllable, or even different syllables. To disambiguate cases open to more than one interpretation, so-called determinatives were introduced, signs that were not pronounced but marked conceptual categories of the words, indicating gods, countries, cities, vessels, birds, trees, etc. For example, the sign for 'bird' was used to mark nouns denoting birds. Determinatives served as a guide for the reader without having spoken counterparts. Functionally, they thus resembled classifiers, which are used, in Chinese and many other modern languages, to classify nouns according to their meaning. The use of word signs, syllabic signs, and determinatives is reminiscent of the way modern Japanese is written. The pictograms eventually became simplified and more abstract, many of them losing their original functions.

Sumerian was a language isolate of a peculiar grammatical structure. Its roots were mostly monosyllabic, but its verbs were conjugated in numerous forms by means of chains of prefixes. Little is known about its pronunciation. Most texts were probably written after Sumerian had ceased to be a spoken language.

Eblaite and Akkadian are old Semitic languages represented in Sumerian writing. In the ancient city of Ebla, Tell Mardikh, southwest of Aleppo in today's Syria, dating from around 2250 BCE, texts have been found that are written in Sumerian cuneiform script but obviously intended to be read in Eblaite (Civil 1984). Eblaite, which is closely related to Akkadian, is considered the oldest written Semitic language.

After the conquest of the Akkad dynasty, Akkadian, a Semitic language, supplanted Sumerian as the major language of Mesopotamia. It was spoken by Assyrians and Babylonians from the 3rd to the 1st millennium BCE on a territory stretching from the Mediterranean to the Persian Gulf. It became the first international language of diplomacy and served for centuries as the lingua franca in the Ancient Near East. It acquired a literary prestige equal to that of Sumerian.

The Sumerian cuneiform script was adopted to Akkadian in the middle of the 2nd millennium BCE. The language is documented in texts covering economy, politics, law, history, religion, scholarship, and letters. It was influenced by Sumerian in direct and intensive language contacts. The writing system was patterned on the Sumerian system. The early writers of Akkadian were probably bilingual and learned cuneiform within the Sumerian scribal tradition.

The alloglottographic nature of the Akkadian writing system is obvious. The Akkadian language was represented by the Sumerian type of writing, i.e. the system of word signs, syllabic signs, and determinatives was taken over. The texts contained numerous Sumerograms, logograms representing whole words, and phonetic symbols from the Sumerian syllabary. Most nouns were preceded by Sumerian determinatives. It is interesting to note that also noun classifiers of modern languages are often copied from other languages. It is sometimes difficult to decide whether a given sign in Akkadian writing is an unpronounced determinative or a Sumerogram intended to be pronounced.

The system was originally not well suited to represent Semitic phonology, partly owing to the syllabic values inherited from the Sumerian script. It was, however, simplified and standardized according to Akkadian needs. The original pictograms were used in a highly abstract way. The Semitic equivalents of many signs were used to represent phonetic values. Syllabic signs based on Akkadian pronunciation were added.

For example, the Sumerian sign for 'king' (*lugal*) was used as a syllabic sign for *šar*, from *šarrum*, the Akkadian word for 'king'.

Most signs could still be interpreted differently depending on the context. In addition to their logographic use, many signs had a function as syllabic phonograms. Readings of this kind are marked with (B) in von Soden's introduction to the Akkadian syllabary (von Soden & Röllig 1991).

During the more than 2000-year-long history of Akkadian, many varieties of it were employed in various places and at various times. The two main dialects were Assyrian in northern Mesopotamina and Babylonian in southern Mesopotamia.

The mixed methods of writing—the mixture of ideographic and phonetic writing—continued until the end of the Babylonian and Assyrian empires, though there were sometimes tendencies to spell out the words more accurately. Old Babylonian was used up to about 1590 BCE, when Sumerian was already defunct. The fact that Babylonian scribes did not have Sumerian as their native language changed the writing system. They had to indicate in more detail how the texts should be read, e.g. verbal forms, which had not been written completely in the old texts. Neo-Assyrian cuneiform was further simplified in the 10th–6th centuries BCE and remained in literary use into Parthian times (250 BCE–226 CE). Akkadian increasingly changed into a non-spoken language, just as Sumerian before it. It expired as a spoken language in the first half of the 1st millennium BCE, ousted by Aramaic, but it remained as a written language for a long time. The last Akkadian texts date from the 1st century CE.

11.2 *Other Codes Represented in Cuneiform Writing*

Cuneiform was used throughout the ancient Near East to write languages that lacked their own writing systems. The script was adapted for writing Hattic, Hurrian, Luvian, Hittite, Urartian, Elamite, West Semitic, etc.

Hittite texts, written in adapted Old Assyrian cuneiform, abound in Sumerograms and Akkadograms, which means that the pronunciation is frequently not clear. The script used in the Hittite scribal schools came from the late Old Babylonian schools in northern Syria, used in Nuzi, Alalakh, and Ugarit. Akkadograms are very common in the oldest Hittite texts, but later become much less frequent. It is uncertain whether they were always read out in Hittite. The numerous Sumerograms are often followed by Hettite endings or longer parts of the end of the word. Most nouns are preceded by determinatives corresponding to the old Sumerian classification. The Hittite readings of the Sumerograms are now mostly known. Exceptions include the words for 'woman' and 'daughter', 'mountain', 'gold', 'silver', and some numerals.

Elamite, a non-Indo-European language that served as an official administrative language of the Persian Empire from the 6th to the 4th century BCE, was written in the Sumerian syllabic script, though it was not related to Sumerian or any of the Semitic and Indo-European neighbors. Ugaritic was written with an alphabet of the Semitic kind that was inspired by cuneiform techniques.

Most adaptations preserved some aspects of the Sumerian script, but the complexity of the system often led to simplified versions. The script was modified according to the requirements of the respective languages. There was a general shift from logography to spelling-based systems, which implied a reduction of alloglottographic devices.

11.3 Old Persian Represented in Elamite Writing

The representation of Old Persian is a continuation of earlier scribal traditions practices. Old Persian was written with a subset of simplified cuneiform characters, a semi-alphabetic syllabary and logograms for frequently occurring words. This script, which was probably never used to represent spoken Old Persian, is known from monumental inscriptions.

A multilingual inscription, attributed to the king Darius and located at Bīsitūn in the Kermānshāh province of Iran, consists of three versions of the same text, written in cuneiform script in the languages Old Persian, Elamite, a non-Indo-European language, and Babylonian, a late form of Akkadian. In his study of this inscription, Gershevitch described what he called Elamite alloglottography of Old Persian. He supposed that Darius uttered his words in Old Persian, whereas the scribes, bilingual Elamite civil servants of the Achaemenid dynasty (ca. 700–330 BCE), wrote them down in Elamite, and read them back to the king, as the inscription says, in Old Persian. The Old Persian version in the inscription is thus a retranslation from Elamite.

Old Persian cuneiform is known only from monumental inscriptions. Probably very few person could write or read it. On the clay tablets of the administriative archives only Elamite is found. It is possible that the script was specially invented for Darius, even if he himself could not read it. For an edition of the inscriptions see Schmitt (1991).

An example of recognizable Elamite influence in the Old Persian text is the Elamite particle *ak*, which means 'and' or serves as a paragraph opener. Since the Old Persian for 'and' is {-ca} or *uta*, 'A and B' was expressed as *A B-ca* or *A-ca B-ca*. The sequence *A B-ca C-ca with-D-ca* 'A and B and C and with D' in the Bīsitūn inscription is explained by Gershevitch as a 'retranslation' of the Elamite recording *A ak B ak C ak with-D*, which represented the Old Persian dictated utterance *A-ca B-ca C-ca with-D* (Langslow 2002: 44–45).

The written Elamite version allowed the reader to recover the original spoken Old Persian message accurately and unambiguously. Elamite was thus higher-ranking in relation to Old Persian in the sense of providing an efficient memorization technique. According to the alloglottographic method, 'written communication within a huge multilingual empire became easy from the Nile to the Indus, by the simplest possible and cleverest device' (Gershevitch 1979: 139).

Semitic scripts have generally provided the basis of the writing systems used for Iranian. Aramaic forms of the Semitic alphabet have been applied to various languages. Aramaic writing, a dominant medium of written communication in the multilingual Achaemenid empire, was also used, from the 5th century BCE onwards, in an alloglottographic way for written texts intended to be read in Old Persian. Bilingual scribes of the addresser would translate the Persian message into Aramaic, and bilingual scribes of the addressee would read it out in Persian or another language. Aramaic as used in the chancelleries was the higher-ranking code in this cultural sense, though it may have been politically subordinate to the varieties spoken by the Iranian rulers and government officials.

11.4   Middle Iranian Represented in Aramaic Writing

Also the writing systems of later Iranian languages involve Aramaic-derived elements. For an overview of Aramaic scripts used for Iranian languages see Skjærvø (1996).

The Pahlavi script was inherited from written Imperial Aramaic as used under the Achaemenids. Pahlavi was earlier sometimes believed to be a mixture of written Imperial Aramaic and spoken Middle Iranian. It is, however, a system of writing rather than a distinct language. It is an ambiguous script with multivalent signs, but it also employs certain devices to specify phonetic values, in particular to render the comprehensive Iranian consonant inventory. Numerous copies of Aramaic words are represented as logograms, Aramaeograms, so-called *huzwārišn* 'interpretations'. For instance, the word for 'dog' is written *KLB* = Aramaic *kalba:*, but pronounced *sag*. Most of the vocabulary and the endings, however, represent spoken Middle Iranian. There is a high degree of ambiguity in this form of writing. For a review of the transliteration problems of Pahlavi see Henning (1958: 126–129). The so-called Pazend system, a reaction to these rather confusing principles, implied the replacement of non-Iranian words with Iranian equivalents through transcription into the phonetically less ambiguous Avestan alphabet.

The Avestan language was an East Iranian language used in Zoroastrian writings. Old Avestan, as reflected in the Zoroastrian sacred book Avesta, is an archaic language, developed around 1000 BCE. Young Avestan was employed to compose new texts even after it had ceased to be a spoken language, probably about 400 BCE. Avestan was a ritual language, the result of a long tradition. It remained in use as a liturgical language of the Avesta canon. The Avestan script was alphabetic. The alphabet, which comprised a large number of letters, was created in the 3rd or 4th century CE. Many of the letters were taken from the Aramaic-derived Pahlavi script. The alphabet was suitable for rendering orally recited texts in a phonetically accurate way, which was considered necessary for the correct form of the liturgy. In general, however, it is unknown to what extent the preserved Avestan texts actually mirror spoken varieties.

Middle Persian, which appeared in the 3rd century CE, may be seen as a continuation of Old Persian, though its phonology, morphology, and syntax are different. It is characterized by analytic structures, loss of genders, cases, and many verb forms (Utas 1991).

Parthian was the language of northeastern and northwestern Iran, based on Northwest Iranian dialects. The Parthian Arsacids, who succeeded the Seleucids, used it along with Persian and Greek as a state language in Parthia. Under the Arsacid dynasty, it spread over all Iran, to Armenia, and to Central Asia. It was widely spoken even in the Sasanid Empire, until the 6th century CE.

The oldest known Arsacid Pahlavi documents, which date back to the 1st century BCE, are normally written alloglottographically in an Aramaic-derived alphabet supplemented by Aramaeograms, which eventually came to be understood as ideograms. Thus, the word for 'bread' would be written *LXM*, Aramaic *lahma:*, but understood as the sign for Iranian *na:n* (Nyberg 1974). Only the Iranian syntactic structure and the Iranian endings added to the Aramaeograms show that the language of the documents cannot be classified as Semitic.

The so-called Awroman documents from the first century CE are almost completely written in the Aramaic way. Only the use of a few participles with additions of phonetic complements suggest that the texts were intended to be read in Parthian (Nyberg 1923).

Sasanian Pahlavi was the official language of the Sasanian empire (3rd–7th centuries CE), the heir of the Parthian Arsacid empire, and probably existed until the 10th century. At the beginning of the Sasanian period, the written administrative language might still have been a variety of Aramaic, but the language in which the texts were read was Middle Persian, pronounced according to an old reading tradition. Persian elements were introduced at an increasing rate. Aramaic words represented by logograms could take on Persian endings and phonetic complements. There were practical aids for scribes, so-called *frahangs* 'word-lists', of which the most important one is a list of Aramaic logograms with their readings in Middle Persian. Book Pahlavi developed in the late Sasanian period and was in use until about 900 CE. Its script differs somewhat from the form used in the inscriptions, e.g. through ambiguity owing to coincidence of several letters.

11.5 Japanese Represented in Chinese Writing

The use of the complex cuneiform systems for alloglottographic representation is similar to the use of a Chinese-derived script to represent Old Japanese. The Japanese *kundoku* practice mentioned above is sometimes cited as an example of alloglottography (Coulmas 1996: 9). The term *kundoku* refers, however, to all types of writing where Chinese characters are used to represent native Japanese words. Alloglottographic representation is characteristic of the old *man'yōgana* system, which was in use from around 600 CE. To employ Chinese characters for writing Japanese, it was necessary not only to represent complete words but also sounds. Sinograms were used as logograms, but also as phonetic characters. Their use as syllabic phonograms and phonetic complements, in particular to represent inflections, resulted in a spelling-based writing system. The phonetization process increasingly disregarded the meanings of the Chinese characters. The sound values were first applied to homonyms and then to any homophonous sequences of phonemes. This led to the rebus principle of 'representing a word by means of the logogram of another which is phonetically similar or homophonous' (Coulmas 1996: 434). This practice is reminiscent of the use of *4U* instead of 'for you', *CU* instead of 'see you', etc., in modern computer jargons. The development later resulted in Japanese phonograms, whose shapes differ essentially from those of the original Chinese characters.

The old Japanese writing system is similar to the Sumerian-derived early Akkadian system. Both used logograms as syllabic phonograms and employed phonetic complements. The study of the similarities may give insights into the origins of early writing systems, i.e. into the general rules that obtain when languages copy logographic scripts (Civil 1984: 75).

The Old Akkadian use of sound values of this kind is limited in comparison to the early Japanese use. Ikeda (2007, 2019) supposes that this is partly a result of the different morphosyntactic and phonotactic structures of the languages.

Firstly, Sumerian and Akkadian have the same basic SOV word order, but Chinese is an SVO language with little morphological marking, whereas Japanese is an SOV language with extensive morphological marking.

Secondly, Sumerian and Akkadian are more similar in their phonotactic structure than Japanese and Chinese are. The fact that Japanese has much stronger phonotactic constraints than Chinese may have been an important reason for Japanese scribes to undertake extensive experiments in how to write Japanese with Chinese characters.

Furthermore, the contact situations were different. The Akkadians lived side by side with Sumerians for a long time, and their language was influenced directly by Sumerian. The early writers were probably bilingual and learned cuneiform under the direct influence of the Sumerian scribal tradition. The

Japanese, however, lived far from China, and there was no massive immigration from China to Japan. Another factor was the strictness of the Akkadian scribal tradition, which made it difficult to develop unconventional values for the characters. Japanese writers of the early literate period were less confined by the Chinese scribal tradition.

As far as these arguments are concerned, it might be suggested that the morphological marking of Japanese might have caused less problems than supposed. Morphological markers, especially case markers, are sometimes omitted in older written Japanese. For example, the nominative marker {-ga}, which is very important in modern Japanese, is omitted in the Sino-Japanese version of a famous piece by Confucius.

(39) Japanese
    a. Sino-Japanese
       Tomo enpō-yori ki-taru ari.
       'A friend (*tomo*) has come (*ki-*) from (*-yori*) a distant place (*enpō*).'

    corresponds to

    b. Modern Japanese
       Tomo-ga   enpō-yori   ki-ta.
       friend-TOP distant.place-from come-PAST
       'A friend has come from a distant place.'

As for the phonotactic constraints, the combination of segmental phonemes in a Chinese syllable is also very restricted. What might be crucial here is not different degrees of phonotactic constraint, but differences in the kinds of constraints. Chinese words, especially Old Chinese ones, are generally monosyllabic, while Japanese words are polysyllabic.

Lastly, the contacts between speakers of Japanese and Chinese may have been much closer than hitherto argued. It is true that there is no historical evidence of massive immigration from China, but for many centuries, private-based trade between the two countries may have been much more active and influential than has been inferred from official documents.

12   A Passive-Active Scale

The five types exemplified above stand for very different kinds of written language intertwining, some representing linguistic codes and others representing text types that involve more than one code. It is thus impossible to analyze them in terms of a unified continuum, a continuous sequence of adjacent types with gliding transitions and distinct extremes.

It seems possible, however, to arrange the types with respect to the roles of the respective higher- and lower-ranking codes. The scale suggested here goes from the most passive roles of low-ranking code to its most active roles in its code interaction with high-ranking code. For the finer distinctions underlying the gradation see the discussions above.

Type 5: This type is positioned at the passive end of the passive-active scale. Low-ranking code is not overtly expressed, but represented by high-ranking code. The type may, however, develop into stages at which low becomes more active, i.e. overtly expressed to a certain extent.

Type 4: Low-ranking code is used to explicate texts in high-ranking code. This type may, however, develop into stages at which low-ranking code becomes more active, operating in its own right, less associated with high-ranking code, though still under its tutor- or mentorship.

Type 3: Low-ranking code operates in its own right, alternating with high-ranking code. This type often represents an inital stage of development of a written literary medium, when writers begin to establish themselves as authors in low-ranking code.

Type 2: Low-ranking code influences high-ranking code by carrying over copies to it, thus playing an active, innovative role.

Type 1: This type is positioned at the active end of the scale, representing plain cases of code copying from high-ranking code with various degrees of adaptation in low-ranking code.

Type 1, subtype 1: This subtype is a preliminary stage that precedes the end of the scale. The copies are not quite incorporated, do not undergo normal adaption, and are thus dealt with as segregated elements, as if they would still belong to a foreign high-ranking code.

Type 1, subtype 2: Low-ranking code incorporates the elements copied from high-ranking code, conventionalizing, adapting, and nativizing them. The codes representing this type does not seem to deserve characteristics such as 'intertwined', 'mixed', or 'hybrid', even if they, as English, may manifest excessive copying.

References

Adamou, Evangelia 2010. Bilingual speech and language ecology in Greek Thrace: Romani and Pomak in contact with Turkish. *Language in Society* 39: 147–171.

Adams, James N. & Janse, Mark & Swain, Simon eds. 2002. *Bilingualism in Ancient Society. Language Contact and the Written Text.* Oxford: Oxford University Press.

Adelaar, Willem F.H. 2004. review of Aikhenvald, Alexandra Y. 2002. *Language Contact in Amazonia.* Oxford: Oxford University Press. Journal of Linguistics 40: 383–387.

Aikhenvald, Alexandra Y. 2001. Areal diffusion, genetic inheritance and problems of subgrouping: A North Arawak case study. In Aikhenvald, Alexandra Y. & Dixon, R.M.W. eds. *Areal Diffusion and Genetic Inheritance: Problems in Comparative Linguistics.* Oxford: Oxford University Press. 167–194.

Aikhenvald, Alexandra Y. 2002. *Language Contact in Amazonia.* Oxford: Oxford University Press.

Aikhenvald, Alexandra Y. 2003. Mechanisms of change in areal diffusion: New morphology and language contact. *Journal of Linguistics* 39: 1–29.

Aikhenvald, Alexandra Y. 2020. Language contact and endangered languages. In Grant, Anthony P. ed. *The Oxford Handbook of Language Contact.* Oxford: Oxford University Press. 172–182.

Aikhenvald, Alexandra & Dixon R[obert]. M.W. eds. 2001. *Areal Diffusion and Genetic Inheritance: Problems in Comparative Linguistics.* Oxford: Oxford University Press.

Austin, Peter K. & Sallabank, Julia 2014. Introduction. In Austin, Peter K. & Sallabank, Julia eds. *Endangered Languages: Beliefs and Ideologies in Language Documentation and Revitalization.* British Academy Scholarship Online. 1–25.

Backus, Ad 1996. *Two in One: Bilingual Speech of Turkish Immigrants in the Netherlands.* Tilburg: Tilburg University Press.

Baki, Ablimit 2012. Language contact between Uyghur and Chinese in Xinjiang: Uyghur elements in Xinjiang Putonghua. *International Journal of Social Linguistics* 215: 41–62.

Bakker, Peter & Marten Mous eds. 1994. *Mixed Languages: 15 Case Studies in Language Intertwining.* Amsterdam: Institute for Functional Research into Languages and Language Use.

Baskakov, Nikolaj A. 1975. *Grammatika xakasskogo jazyka* [Grammar of Khakas]. Moskva: Nauka.

Baumgarten, Jean 2005. *Introduction to Old Yiddish Literature.* Edited and translated by Jerold C. Frakes. Oxford: Oxford University Press.

Bechert, Heinz 2005. *Eine regionale hochsprachliche Tradition in Südasien: Sanskrit-Literatur bei den buddhistischen Singhalesen* [A Regional High Language Tradition in South Asia: Sanskrit Literature Among the Buddhist Sinhalese]. (Österreichische

Akademie der Wissenschaften, philosophisch-historische Klasse, Sitzungsberichte 718; Veröffentichungen zu den Sprachen und Kulturen Südasiens 37.) Wien: Verlag der Österreichischen Akademie der Wissenschaften.

Benzing, Johannes 1955. *Lamutische Grammatik* [Lamut Grammar]. Wiesbaden: Harrassowitz.

Berberian, Haig 1964. La litérature arméno-turque [The Armeno-Turkic literature.] In Bazin, Louis & Bombaci Alessio & Deny, Jean & Gökbilgin, Tayyib & İz, Fahir & Scheel, Helmuth eds. 1964. *Philologiae Turcicae Fundamenta* 2. Aquis Mattiacis: Steiner. 809–819.

Berta, Árpád 1989. *Lautgeschichte der tatarischen Dialekte* [Sound History of the Tatar Dialects]. Szeged: University of Szeged.

Birnbaum, Solomon A. 1979. *Yiddish: A Survey and a Grammar*. Toronto: University of Toronto Press.

Blondheim, David Simon 1926a. Contribution à l'étude de la poésie judéo-française [Contribution to the study of Judeo-French poetry]. *Revue des Études Juives* 82: 381–389.

Blondheim, David Simon 1926b. Poésies judéo-françaises. [Judeo-French poetry]. *Romania* 52: 20–22.

Böhl, Franz Marius Theodor 1909. Die Sprache der Amarnabriefe mit besonderer Berücksichtigung der Kanaanismen [The Language of the Amarna Letters with Special Reference to Canaanisms]. (Leipziger Semitistische Studien 5:2.) Leipzig: J.C. Hinrich.

Bodrogligeti, András J.E. 2001. *A Grammar of Chagatay*. (Languages of the World. Materials 155.) Munich: Lincom Europa.

Bohnacker, Ute & Karakoç, Birsel 2020. Subordination in children acquiring Turkish as a heritage language in Sweden. In Bayram, Fatih ed. *Studies in Turkish as a Heritage Language*. (Studies in Bilingualism 60.) Amsterdam: John Benjamins. 155–204.

Browne, Edward Granville 1906. *A Literary History of Persia* 2. London: T. Fisher Unwin.

Brendemoen, Bernt 1993. Pronominalsyntax in den türkischen Schwarzmeerdialekten. Syntaktische Innovation oder Archaismus? [Pronominal syntax in the Turkish Black Sea dialects. Innovation or archaism?] In Laut, Jens Peter & Röhrborn, Klaus eds. *Sprach- und Kulturkontakte der türkischen Völker*. (Veröffentlichungen der Societas Uralo-Altaica 37.) Wiesbaden: Harrassowitz. 51–73.

Bulut, Christiane 2006. Turkish elements in spoken Kurmanji. In Boeschoten, Hendrik & Johanson, Lars eds. *Turkic Languages in Contact*. (Turcologica 61.) Wiesbaden: Harrassowitz. 95–121.

Caferoğlu, Ahmed 1964. Die aserbeidschanische Literatur [Azerbaijani literature]. In Bazin, Louis & Bombaci Alessio & Deny, Jean & Gökbilgin, Tayyib & İz, Fahir & Scheel, Helmuth eds. 1964. *Philologiae Turcicae Fundamenta* 2. Aquis Mattiacis: Steiner. 635–699.

REFERENCES

Civil, Miguel 1984. Bilingualism in logographically written languages: Sumerian in Ebla. In Cagni, Luigi ed. *Il bilinguismo a Ebla. Atti del convegno internazionale, Napoli, 19–22 aprile, 1982.* Naples. 75–97.

Clyne, Michael 2003. *Dynamics of Language Contact: English and Immigrant Languages.* (Cambridge Approaches to Language Contact.) Cambridge: Cambridge University Press.

Colonna, Francesco 1499. *Poliphili Hypnerotomachia, ubi humana omnia non nisi sōmnium esse ostendit, atque obiter plurima scitu sanequam digna commemorat.* [The Hypnerotomachia of Poliphilus, in which He Shows that All Things are Human Except that There is a Dream]. Venedig: Aldus manutius [Reprint 1904. London: Methuen.]

Comrie, Bernard 1981. *The Languages of the Soviet Union.* Cambridge: Cambridge University Press.

Comrie, Bernard 1995. Review of Johanson, Lars 1992. *Strukturelle Faktoren in türkischen Sprachkontakten* [Structural Factors in Turkic Linguistic Contacts]. (Sitzungsberichte der Wissenschaftlichen Gesellschaft an der J.W. Goethe-Universität Frankfurt am Main 29: 5.) Stuttgart: Steiner. *Rivista di Linguistica* 7: 391–394.

Comrie, Bernard 2002. Introduction. In Johanson, Lars 2002c. *Structural Factors in Turkic Language Contacts.* London: Curzon. vii–xii.

Corne, Chris 1995. A contact-induced and vernacularized language: How Melanesian is Tayo? In Baker, Philip ed. *From Contact to Creole and Beyond.* London: University of Westminster Press. 121–148.

Coulmas, Florian 1996. *The Blackwell Encyclopedia of Writing Systems.* Oxford: Blackwell.

Csató, Éva Á. 1998. Should Karaim be 'purer' than other European languages? *Studia Turcologica Cracoviensia* 5: 81 89.

Csató, Éva Á. 2000. Syntactic code-copying in Karaim. In Dahl, Östen & Koptjevskaja-Tamm, Maria eds. *The Circum-Baltic Languages: Their Typology and Contacts* 1–2. Amsterdam: John Benjamins. 265–277.

Csató, Éva Á. 2006. Copying word order properties. In Boeschoten, Hendrik & Johanson, Lars eds. *Turkic Languages in Contact.* Wiesbaden: Harrassowitz. 152–157.

Csató, Éva Á. 2011. A typological coincidence: Word order properties in Trakai Karaim biblical translations. In Rona, Bengisu & Erguvanlı-Taylan, Eser eds. *Puzzles of Language. Essays in Honour of Karl Zimmer.* (Turcologica 86.) Wiesbaden: Harrassowitz. 169–186.

Csató, Éva Á. 2012. On the sustainability of inflectional morphology. In Johanson, Lars & Robbeets, Martine eds. *Copies versus Cognates in Bound Morphology.* Leiden & Boston: Brill. 371–380.

Csató, Éva Á. & Johanson, Lars & Róna-Tas, András & Utas, Bo eds. 2016. *Turks and Iranians: A Common Historical and Linguistic Heritage.* (Turcologica 105.) Harrassowitz: Wiesbaden.

Csató, Éva Á. & Johanson, Lars 2020. The Northwestern Turkic (Kipchak) languages. In Robbeets, Martine & Savelyev, Alexander eds. *The Oxford Guide of Transeurasian Languages*. Oxford: Oxford University Press. 370–391.

Csató, Éva Á. & Menz, Astrid 2018. On the linguistic distances between Gagauz and Karaim. *Turkic Languages* 22: 43–62.

Dankoff, Robert 1990. *Evliya Çelebi in Bitlis. The Relevant Section of the Seyahatname Edited with Translation, Commentary and Introduction*. Leiden & New York & København & Köln: E.J. Brill.

Devereux, Robert 1966. *Muhākamat al-lughatain by Mir ʿAli Shir. Introduction, Translation and Notes* [Judgment of the Two Languages]. Leiden: E.J. Brill.

Dixon, Robert M.W. 1997. *The Rise and Fall of Languages*. Cambridge: Cambridge University Press.

Doerfer, Gerhard 1967. *Türkische Lehnwörter im Tadschikischen* [Turkic Loanwords in Tajik]. Wiesbaden: Steiner.

Doerfer, Gerhard 1985. The Mongol-Tungus connection. *Language Research* 21: 135–144.

Dolatkhah, Sohrab & Csató, Éva Á. & Karakoç, Birsel 2016. On the marker -(y)akï in the Kashkay variety spoken in the Jamehbuzurgi subtribe of the Amaleh tribe. In Csató, Éva Á. & Johanson, Lars & Róna-Tas, András & Utas, Bo eds. 2016. *Turks and Iranians: A Common Historical and Linguistic Heritage*. (Turcologica 105.) Harrassowitz: Wiesbaden. 283–295.

Dolatkhah, Sohrab 2023. Kashkay. In Johanson, Lars ed. *Encyclopedia of Turkic Languages and Linguistics Online*. Brill.

Eckmann, János 1966. *Chagatay Manual*. (Indiana University Uralic and Altaic Series 60.) Bloomington: Indiana University Press.

Edgerton, Franklin 1953. *Buddhist Hybrid Sanskrit Grammar and Dictionary 1–2*. New Haven. [Reprint 2004. Munshiram Manoharlal Publishers.] Kommissionsverlag: Motilal Banarsidass, Delhi.]

Elwert, Wilhelm Theodor 1960. L'emploi de langues étrangères comme procédé stylistique [The use of foreign languages as a stylistic device]. *Revue de Littérature Comparée* 43: 409–437.

Elwert, Wilhelm Theodor 1972. Fremdsprachliche Einsprengsel in der Dichtung [Sprinkles of foreign language in the poetry]. In Haarmann, Harald et al. eds. *Festschrift Wilhelm Giese. Beiträge zur Romanistik und allgemeinen Sprachwissenschaft*. Hamburg: Buske. 513–545.

Erdal, Marcel 1991. *Old Turkic Word Formation. A Functional Approach to the Lexicon.* (Turcologica 7.) Wiesbaden: Harrassowitz.

Erdal, Marcel 1997. Review of Lars Johanson, Strukturelle Faktoren in türkischen Sprachkontakten [Structural Factors in Turkic Language Contacts, Stuttgart 1992. *Mediterranean Language Review* 9/10: 227–234.

Fewster, Penelope 2002. Bilingualism in Roman Egypt. In Adams, James N. & Janse, Mark & Swain, Simon eds. 2002. *Bilingualism in Ancient Society. Language Contact and the Written Text*. Oxford: Oxford University Press. 220–245.

Fisiak, Jacek ed. *Historical Morphology*. The Hague: Mouton.

Forster, Leonard 1970. *The Poet's Tongues: Multilingualism in Literature*. Cambridge: Cambridge University Press.

Fragner, Bert G. 2006. Das Persische als Hegemonialsprache in der islamischen Geschichte: Überlegungen zur Definition eines innerislamischen Kulturraums [Persian as a hegemonic language in Islamic history: Reflections on the definition of an inner-Islamic cultural sphere]. In Johanson, Lars & Bulut, Christiane eds. *Turkic-Iranian Contact Areas. Historical and linguistic aspects*. (Turcologica 62.) Wiesbaden: Harrassowitz. 39–48.

Gabain, Annemarie von 1950^2. *Alttürkische Grammatik* [Old Turkic Grammar]. Leipzig: Harrassowitz.

Gardani, Francesco 2012. Plural across inflection and derivation, fusion and agglutination. In Johanson, Lars & Robbeets, Martine eds. *Copies Versus Cognates in Bound Morphology*. Leiden & Boston: Brill. 71–97.

Gargesh, Ravinder 2008. *Indian English. Phonology*. Berlin: De GruyterMouton.

Gershevitch, Ilya 1979. The alloglottography of Old Persian. *Transactions of the Philological Society* 1979: 114–190.

Gianto, Agustinus 1990. *Word Order Variation in the Akkadian of Byblos*. (Studia Pohl 15.) Roma: Editrice Pontificio Istituto Biblico.

Gorelova, Liliya M. 2002. *Manchu Grammar*. (Handbook of Oriental Studies 8. Uralic and Central Asian Studies 7.) Leiden: Brill.

Griffiths, Paul J. 1981. Buddhist Hybrid English: Some notes on philology and hermeneutics for Buddhologists. *Journal of the International Association of Buddhist Studies*, 4/2: 17–32.

Grünewald, August 1908. *Die lateinischen Einschiebsel in den deutschen Gedichten von der Mitte des XI. bis gegen das Ende des XII. Jahrhunderts* [The Latin Insertions in the German Poems from the Middle of the 11th until the End of the 12th Century.] Göttingen: E.A. Huth.

Haenisch, Erich 1961. *Mandschu-Grammatik* [Manchu Grammar]. Leipzig: Verlag Enzyklopädie.

Heine, Bernd 2006. *Contact-induced Word Order Change without Word Order Change*. (Working Papers in Multilingualism, Series B, 76.) Universität Hamburg: Sonderforschungsbereich Mehrsprachigkeit.

Heine, Bernd & Kuteva, Tania 2003. On contact-induced grammaticalization. *Studies in Language* 27: 529–572.

Heine, Bernd & Kuteva, Tania 2005. *Language Contact and Grammatical Change*. Cambridge: Cambridge University Press.

Helander, Hans 2004. *Neo-Latin Literature in Sweden in the period 1620–1720. Stylistics, Vocabulary and Characteristic Ideas.* (Studia Latina Upsaliensia.) Uppsala: Uppsala University Library.

Henning, Walter B. 1958. Altiranisch [Old Iranic]. In *Handbuch der Orientalistik 1: 4. Iranistik 1. Linguistik.* Leiden-Köln: Brill. 20–130.

Henrici, Emil 1913. *Sprachmischung in älterer Dichtung Deutschlands* [Language Mixing in Older German Poetry]. Berlin: Victor Fischer.

von Hinüber, Oskar 1978. Pali as an artificial language. *Indologica Taurinensia* 10: 133–140.

von Hinüber, Oskar 1983. Notes on the Pali tradition in Burma. (Beiträge zur Überlieferungsgeschichte des Buddhismus in Birma 1.) *Nachrichten der Akademie der Wissenschaften in Göttingen 1. Philologisch-historische Klasse* 3: 65–79.

Igla, Birgit 1996. *Das Romani von Ajia Varvara: Deskriptive und historisch-vergleichende Darstellung eines Zigeunerdialektes* [The Romany of Ajia Varvara: Descriptive and Historical-comparative Treatment of a Gypsy Dialect]. Wiesbaden: Harrassowitz.

Ikeda, Jun 2007. Early Japanese and early Akkadian writing systems. A contrastive survey of 'Kunogenesis'. Paper given at the conference *Origins of Early Writing Systems* (October 6, 2007). Beijing: Peking University.

Ikeda, Jun 2019. Relational units in cuneiform writing: Two cases of comparative graphemics. In Nakata, Ichiro et al. eds. 2019. *Prince of the Orient: Ancient Near Eastern Studies in Memory of H.I.H. Prince Takahito Mikasa.* Tokyo: The Society for Near Eastern Studies in Japan. 259–268.

Izre'el, Shlomo 1978. The Gezer letters of the El-Amarna archive—linguistic analysis. *Israel Oriental Studies* 8: 13–90.

Izre'el, Shlomo 1991. *Amurru Akkadian: A Linguistic Study.* Atlanta, Ga.: Scholars Press.

Izre'el, Shlomo 2005^2. *Canaano-Akkadian.* (Languages of the World/Materials 82.) München: LINCOM Europa.

Jacobs, Neil G. 2005. *Yiddish: A Linguistic Introduction.* Cambridge: Cambridge University Press.

Jespersen, Otto 1922. *Language. Its Nature, Development and Origin.* London: George Allen & Unwin.

Johanson, Lars 1971. *Aspekt im Türkischen. Vorstudien zu einer Beschreibung des türkeitürkischen Aspektsystems* [Aspect in Turkish. Preliminary Studies for the Description of the Turkish Aspect System]. Uppsala: Almqvist & Wiksell.

Johanson, Lars 1974. Zur Syntax der alttürkischen Kausativa [On the syntax of the Old Turkic causatives]. *Zeitschrift der Deutschen Morgenländischen Gesellschaft, Supplement* 2: 529–540.

Johanson, Lars 1975a. Some remarks on Turkic "hypotaxis". *Ural-Altaische Jahrbücher* 7, 104–118. [Reprinted in Johanson, Lars 1991. *Linguistische Beiträge zur Gesamtturkolo-*

gie [Linguistic Contributions to Comparative Turcology]. Budapest: Akadémiai Kiadó: 210–224.]

Johanson, Lars 1975b. Gesprochenes Türkisch als Forschungsobjekt [Spoken Turkish as a research object]. *Materialia Turcica* 1: 1–8.

Johanson, Lars 1976. Das tschuwaschische Aoristthema [The Chuvash aorist theme]. *Orientalia Suecana* 23–24: 106–158. [Also in Johanson, Lars 1991. *Linguistische Beiträge zur Gesamtturkologie* [Linguistic Contributions to Comparative Turcology]. Budapest: Akadémiai Kiadó 117–169.]

Johanson, Lars 1988. Iranian elements in Azeri Turkish. In Yarshater, Ehsan ed. *Encyclopedia Iranica* 3, London & New York: Routledge & Kegan Paul. 248b–251a.

Johanson, Lars 1989. Substandard und Sprachwandel im Türkischen. [Substandard and language change in Turkic]. In Holtus, Günter & Radtke, Edgar eds. *Sprachlicher Substandard 2. Standard und Substandard in der Sprachgeschichte und in der Grammatik*. (Konzepte der Sprach- und Literaturwissenschaft 44.) Tübingen: Niemeyer. 83–112.

Johanson, Lars 1991a. *Linguistische Beiträge zur Gesamtturkologie* [Linguistic Contributions to Comparative Turcology]. Budapest: Akadémiai Kiadó.

Johanson, Lars 1991b. Zur Sprachentwicklung der "Turcia Germanica" [On the language development of "Turcia Germanica"]. In Baldauf, Ingeborg & Kreiser, Klaus & Tezcan, Semih eds. *Türkische Sprachen und Literaturen. Materialien der Ersten Deutschen Turkologen-Konferenz Bamberg, 3.–6. Juli 1987*. Wiesbaden: Harrassowitz. 199–212.

Johanson, Lars 1992. *Strukturelle Faktoren in türkischen Sprachkontakten* [Structural Factors in Turkic Linguistic Contacts]. (Sitzungsberichte der Wissenschaftlichen Gesellschaft an der J.W. Goethe-Universität Frankfurt am Main 29: 5.) Stuttgart: Steiner.

Johanson, Lars 1993a. Rūmī and the birth of Turkish poetry. *Journal of Turkology* 1: 23–37.

Johanson, Lars 1993b. Code-copying in immigrant Turkish. In Extra, Guus. & Verhoeven, Ludo eds. *Immigrant Languages in Europe*. Clevedon & Philadelphia & Adelaide: Multilingual Matters. 197–221.

Johanson, Lars 1993c. Typen kausaler Satzverbindungen im Türkischen [Types of causal clause combining in Turkic]. *Journal of Turkology* 1: 213–267.

Johanson, Lars 1994a. Formal aspects of ʻaruḍ versification. In Johanson, Lars & Utas, Bo eds. *Arabic Prosody and its Applications in Muslim Poetry*. Stockholm: Swedish Research Institute in Istanbul. 7–16.

Johanson, Lars 1994b. Funktion, Kompetenz und Etymon. Bemerkungen zu einer ostalttürkischen Wortbildungslehre [Function, competence and etymon. Notes on East Old Turkic word formation]. *Central Asiatic Journal* 160–178.

Johanson, Lars 1995. On Turkic converb clauses. In Haspelmath, Martin & König, Ekkehard eds. *Converbs in Cross-linguistic Perspective. Structure and Meaning of Adverbial Verb Forms—Adverbial Participles, Gerunds.* (Empirical approaches to language typology 13.) Berlin & New York: De Gruyter Mouton. 313–347.

Johanson, Lars 1996a. On Bulgarian and Turkic indirectives. In Boretzky, Norbert & Enninger, Werner & Stolz, Thomas eds. *Areale, Kontakte, Dialekte. Sprache und ihre Dynamik in mehrsprachigen Situationen* (Bochum-Essener Beiträge zur Sprachwandelforschung 24.) Bochum: Brockmeyer. 84–94.

Johanson, Lars 1996b. Kopierte Satzjunktoren im Türkischen [Copies of clause junctors in Turkic]. *Sprachtyplogie und Universalienforschung* 9: 39–94.

Johanson, Lars 1997a. Kopien russischer Konjunktionen in türkischen Sprachen [Copies of Russian conjunctions in Turkic languages]. In Huber, Dieter & Worbs, Erika eds. *Ars transferendi. Sprache, Übersetzung, Interkulturalität.* Frankfurt: Peter Lang. 115–121.

Johanson, Lars 1997b. A grammar of the "lingua turcica agemica". In Kellner–Heinkele, Barbara & Zieme, Peter eds. *Studia Ottomanica. Festgabe für György Hazai zum 65. Geburtstag.* (Veröffentlichungen der Societas Uralo-Altaica 47.) Wiesbaden: Harrassowitz. 87–101.

Johanson, Lars 1998a. The structure of Turkic. In Johanson, Lars & Csató, Éva Á. eds. 1998. *The Turkic Languages.* London: Routledge. 30–66.

Johanson, Lars 1998b. Code-copying in Irano-Turkic. *Language Sciences* 20: 325–337.

Johanson, Lars 1998c. Zum Kontakteinfluß türkischer Indirektive [On the contact influence of Turkic indirectives]. In Demir, Nurettin & Taube, Erika eds. *Turkologie Heute. Tradition und Perspektive.* Wiesbaden: Harrassowitz. 141–150.

Johanson, Lars 1999a. The dynamics of code-copying in language encounters. In Brendemoen, Bernt & Lanza, Elizabeth & Ryen, Else eds. *Language Encounters Across Time and Space.* Oslo: Novus Press. 37–62.

Johanson, Lars 1999b. Frame-changing code-copying in immigrant varieties. In Extra, Guus & Verhoeven, Ludo eds. *Bilingualism and Migration* (Studies on Language Acqusition 14.) Berlin & New York: De Gruyter Mouton. 247–260.

Johanson, Lars 2000a. Linguistic convergence in the Volga area. In Gilbers, Dicky & Nerbonne, John & Schaeken, Jos eds. *Languages in Contact.* (Studies in Slavic and General Linguistics 28.) Amsterdam & Atlanta: Rodopi. 165–178.

Johanson, Lars 2000b. Attractiveness and relatedness: Notes on Turkic language contacts. In Good, Jeff & Yu, Alan C.L. eds. *Special Session on Caucasian, Dravidian, and Turkic Linguistics. Proceedings of the Twenty-Fifth Annual Meeting of the Berkeley Linguistic Society, February 12–15, 1999.* Berkeley: Berkeley Linguistics Society. 87–89.

Johanson, Lars 2002a. Contact-induced linguistic change in a code-copying framework. In Jones, Mari C. & Esch, Edith eds. *Language Change: The Interplay of Internal, External and Extra-linguistic Factors.* (Contributions to the Sociology of Language 86.) Berlin: De Gruyter Mouton. 285–313.

REFERENCES

Johanson, Lars 2002b. Do languages die of 'structuritis'? The role of code-copying in language endangerment. *Italian Journal of Linguistics* 14: 249–270.

Johanson, Lars 2002c. *Structural Factors in Turkic Language Contacts.* London: Curzon. [With an introduction by Bernard Comrie.]

Johanson, Lars 2005a. Converging codes in Iranian, Semitic and Turkic. In Csató, Éva Á. & Isaksson, Bo & Jahani, Carina eds. *Linguistic Convergence and Areal Diffusion. Case Studies from Iranian, Semitic and Turkic.* London & New York: RoutledgeCurzon. 3–31.

Johanson, Lars 2005b. On copying grammatical meaning. *Sprachtypologie und Universalienforschung* 58: 75–83.

Johanson, Lars 2008a. Remodeling grammar copying, conventionalism, grammaticalization. In Siemund, Peter & Kintana, Noemi eds. *Language Contact and Contact Languages.* (Hamburg Studies on Multilingualism 7.) Amsterdam: Benjamins. 61–79.

Johanson, Lars 2008b. Case and contact linguistics. In Malchukov, Andrej & Spencer, Andrew eds. *The Oxford Handbook of Case.* Oxford: Oxford University Press. 249–270.

Johanson, Lars 2011. Grammaticalizaton in Turkic languages. In Narrog, Heiko & Heine, Bernd eds. *The Oxford Handbook of Grammaticalization.* Oxford: Oxford University Press. 752–761.

Johanson, Lars 2013a. Written language intertwining. In Bakker, Peter & Matras, Yaron eds. *Contact Languages. A Comprehensive Guide.* Boston & Berlin: De Gruyter Mouton. 273–331.

Johanson, Lars 2013b. Isomorphic processes: Grammaticalization and copying of grammatical elements. In Robbeets, Martine & Cuyckens, Hubert eds. *Shared Grammaticalization. With Special Focus on the Transeurasian Langugages.* Amsterdam & Philadelphia: John Benjamins. 101–109.

Johanson, Lars 2014a. Intimate family reunions: Code-copying between Turkic relatives. In Besters-Dilger, Juliane & Dermarkar, Cynthia & Pfänder, Stefan & Rabus, Achim eds. *Congruence in Contact-induced Language Change. Language Families, Typological Resemblance, and Similarity* (linguae & litterae 27.) Berlin & Boston: De Gruyter. 137–145.

Johanson, Lars 2014b. A Yakut copy of a Tungusic viewpoint aspect paradigm. In Robbeets, Martine & Bisang, Walter eds. *Paradigm Change in the Transeurasian Languages and Beyond.* Amsterdam & Philadelphia: John Benjamins. 235–242.

Johanson Lars, 2021. *Turkic.* (Cambridge Language Surveys). Cambridge: Cambridge University Press.

Johanson, Lars 2022^2. The structure of Turkic. In Johanson, Lars & Csató, Éva Á. eds. 2022^2. *The Turkic Languages.* (Routledge Language Family Series.) New York & London: Routledge. 26–59.

Johanson, Lars & Bulut, Christiane eds. 2006. *Turkic-Iranian Contact Areas. Historical and Linguistic Aspects.* (Turcologica 62.) Wiesbaden: Harrassowitz.

Johanson, Lars & Csató, Éva Á. 2022. Code Copying and the strength of languages. In Storch, Anne & Dixon, R.M.W. eds. *The Art of Language.* Leiden & Boston: Brill. 302–315.

Johanson, Lars & Robbeets, Martine 2012. eds. *Copies vs. Cognates in Bound Morphology.* Leiden & Boston: Brill.

Johanson, Lars & Robbeets, Martine 2012. Bound morphology in common: Copy or cognate? In Johanson, Lars & Robbeets, Martine 2012. eds. *Copies vs. Cognates in Bound Morphology.* Leiden & Boston: Brill. 3–22.

Johanson, Lars & Bo Utas eds. 1994. *Arabic Prosody and its Applications in Muslim Poetry. Swedish Research Institute in Istanbul.* (Transactions 5.) Stockholm: Swedish Research Institute in Istanbul.

Joseph, Brian D. 2012. A variationist solution to apparent copying. In Johanson, Lars & Robbeets, Martine 2012. eds. *Copies vs. Cognates in Bound Morphology.* Leiden & Boston: Brill. 151–164.

Karakoç, Birsel 2009. Notes on subject markers and copular forms in Turkish and in some Turkic varieties of Iran: A comparative study. *Turkic Languages* 13: 208–224.

Karakoç, Birsel 2019. Predicative possession in Oghuz and Kipchak Turkic languages. In Johanson, Lars & Mazzitelli, Lidia Federica & Nevskaya, Irina eds. *Possession in Languages of Europe and North and Central Asia.* (Studies in Language Companion Series 206.) Amsterdam: John Benjamins. 125–148.

Karakoç, Birsel & Herkenrath, Annette 2019. Understanding retold stories: The marking of unwitnessed events in bilingual Turkish. *Turkic Languages* 23: 81–121.

Katz, Dovid 1987. *Grammar of the Yiddish Language.* London: Gerald Duckworth & Co.

Kıral, Filiz 2001. *Das gesprochene Aserbaidschanisch von Iran: Eine Studie zu den syntaktischen Einflüssen des Persischen* [Spoken Azeri of Iran. A Study on the Persian Syntactic Influences]. (Turcologica 43.) Wiesbaden: Harrassowitz.

Kloss, Heinz 1952. *Die Entwicklung neuer germanischer Kultursprachen von 1800 bis 1950* [The development of New Germanic Culture Languages from 1800 to 1950]. (Schriftenreihe des Goethe-Instituts 1.) München: Pohl & Co.

Knudtzon, Jørgen Alexander 1907–1915. *Die El-Amarna-Tafeln. Umschrift, Übersetzung und Glossar 1–2* [The El Amarna Tablets. Transcription, Translation, and Glossary]. (Vorderasiatische Bibliothek, 2.) Leipzig: Hinrichs.

Köprülü, M. Fuad 1964. La métrique ʿarūż dans la poésie turque [The ʿarūż metric in Turkic poetry]. In Bazin, Louis & Bombaci Alessio & Deny, Jean & Gökbilgin, Tayyib & İz, Fahir & Scheel, Helmuth eds. 1964. *Philologiae Turcicae Fundamenta* 2. Aquis Mattiacis: Steiner. 252–266.

Kossmann, Maarten G. 1989. The case system of West-Semitized Amarna Akkadian. *Jaarbericht Ex Oriente Lux* 30: 38–60.

Kowalski, Tadeusz 1929. *Karaimische Texte im Dialekt von Troki*. [Karaim Texts in the Dialect of Troki]. Warszawa: L'Académie Polonaise des Sciences et des Lettres.

Kowalski, Tadeusz 1934. Osmanisch-türkische Dialekte [Ottoman Turkish dialects]. *Enzyklopaedie des Islam* 4. Leiden: Brill. 991–1010.

Langslow, David R. 2002. Approaching bilingualism in corpus languages. In Adams, James N. & Janse, Mark & Swain, Simon eds. *Bilingualism in Ancient Society. Language Contact and the Wittten Word*. Oxford: Oxford University Press. 23–51.

Lazar, Moshé 1971. Epithalames bilingues hébraïco-romans dans deux manuscrits du xve siècle [Bilingual Hebrew-Romance epithalamus in two 15th-century manuscripts]. In Cluzel, Irénée-Marcel & Pirot, François eds. *Mélanges de philologie romane: Dédiés à la mémoire de Jean Boutière* 1. Liège: Editions Soledi. 333–346.

Lewis, Geoffrey 1999. *The Turkish Language Reform: A Catastrophic Success*. Oxford: Oxford University Press.

Li, Charles N. & Thompson, Sandra A. 1974. Historical change of word order: A case study in Chinese and its implications. In Anderson, John M. & Jones, Charles eds. *Historical Linguistics*. Amsterdam: NorthHolland Publishing Company. 199–217.

Lutz, Angelika 2012. Norse influence on English in the light of general contact linguistics. In Hegedűs, Irén & Fodor, Alexandra eds. *English Historical Linguistics 2010: Selected Papers from the Sixteenth International Conference on English Historical Linguistics (ICEHL 16), Pécs, 23–27 August 2010*. Amsterdam: John Benjamins. 15–42.

Malmqvist, Göran 1979. Berhard Karlgren in memoriam. *Journal of Chinese Linguistics* 7: 42–44.

Mansuroğlu, Mecdud 1954. The rise and development of written Turkish in Anatolia. *Oriens* 7: 250–264.

Matras, Yaron 2006. Layers of convergent syntax in Macedonian Turkish. In Boeschoten, Hendrik & Johanson, Lars eds. *Turkic Languages in Contact*. Wiesbaden: Harrassowitz. 46–62.

Matras, Yaron 2009. *Language Contact*. (Cambridge Textbooks in Linguistics.) Cambridge: Cambridge University Press.

Matras, Yaron & Peter Bakker eds. 2003. *The Mixed Language Debate: Theoretical and Empirical Advances*. Berlin: De Gruyter.

Meisig, Konrad 2008a. Buddhist Chinese. Religiolect and metalanguage. *Mitteilungen für Anthropologie und Religionsgeschichte* 19: 91–100. Münster: Ugarit-Verlag.

Meisig, Konrad 2008b. Review of Bechert, Heinz 2005. *Eine regionale hochsprachliche Tradition in Südasien: Sanskrit-Literatur bei den buddhistischen Singhalesen*. Wien: Verlag der Österreichischen Akademie der Wissenschaften. *Internationales Asienforum* 39: 363–366.

Menges, Karl H. 1943. The Tungus tense in *-ra*. *Language* 19: 237–251.

Menges, Karl H. 1968. *The Turkic Languages and Peoples. An Introduction to Turkic Studies*. (Ural-Altaische Bibliothek 15.) Wiesbaden: Harrassowitz.

Menz, Astrid 2001. Gagauz right-branching propositions introduced by the element *ani*. *Turkic Languages* 5: 234–244.

Miller, Roy Andrew 1967. *The Japanese Language*. Chicago: University of Chicago Press.

Miller, Roy Andrew 1982. Altaic origins of the Japanese verb classes. In Arbeitman, Yoel L. & Bomhard, Allan R. eds. *Bono Homini Donum: Essays in Historical Linguistics in Memory of J. Alexander Kerns*. Amsterdam: John Benjamins. 845–880.

Miller, Roy Andrew 1983. Japanese evidence for some Altaic denominal verb-stem derivational suffixes. *Acta Orientalia Hungarica* 36: 391–403.

Miller, Roy Andrew 1991a. Anti-Altaists contra Altaists. *Ural-Altaic Yearbook* 63: 5–62.

Miller, Roy Andrew 1991b. Genetic connections among the Altaic languages. In Lamb, Sydney M. & Mitchell, Douglas E. eds. *Sprung from Some Common Source. Investigations into the Prehistory of Languages*. Stanford: Stanford University Press. 298–327.

Miller, Roy Andrew 1996. *Languages and History. Japanese, Korean, and Altaic*. Bangkok: Orchid Press.

Minegishi, Akira 1986. *Hentai Kambun* [Hentai Chinese Writing]. Tokyo: Tôkyôdô.

Moran, William L. 1950. *A Syntactical Study of the Dialect of Byblos as Reflected in the Amarna Tablets*. PhD dissertation. John Hopkins University, Baltimore.

Mosel, Ulrike 2012. Creating educational materials in language documentation projects: Creating innovative resources for linguistic research. In Seifart, Frank et al. eds. *Potentials of Language Documentation: Methods, Analyses, and Utilization*. Honolulu: University of Hawaaiʻi Press. 111–117.

Mosel, Ulrike 2014. Corpus linguistic and documentary approaches in writing a grammar of a previously undescribed language. In Nakayama, Toshihide & Rice, Keren eds. *The Art and Practice of Grammar Writing*. Honolulu: University of Hawaaiʻi Press. 135–157.

Müller, Otto 1919. *Das lateinische Enschiebsel in der französischen Literatur des Mittelalters* [The Latin Insertion in French Literature of the Middle Ages]. PhD thesis. University of Zürich.

Musaev, Kenesbaj M. 1964. *Grammatika karaimskogo jazyka. Fonetika i morfologija* [Grammar of the Karaim Language. Phonetics and Morphology]. Moskva: Nauka.

Muyskin, Peter 2000. *Bilingual Speech. A Typology of Code Mixing*. Cambridge: Cambridge University Press.

Németh, Julius 1953. Zur Kenntnis der Mischsprachen. Das doppelte Sprachsystem des Osmanischem [On the knowledge of the mixed languages. The double language system of Ottoman]. *Acta Linguistica Academiae Scientiarum Hungaricae* 3: 159–199.

Nevins, Andrew & Vaux, Bert 2004. Consonant harmony in Karaim. In Csirmaz, Anikó & Lee, Youngjoo & Walter, MaryAnn eds. *Proceedings of WAFL 1: Workshop on Altaic in Formal Linguistics*. Cambridge, Ma.: Massachussetts Institute of Technology. 175–194.

Numamoto, Katsuaki 2008. Nihon ni okeru kunten-shiryoo no tenkai: shutoshite ondoku no kanten kara. [The development of *kunten*-data in Japan: Mainly from the viewpoint of *ondoku.*] In Nakamura, Shunsaku et al. eds. *Kundoku-ron.* Tokyo: Bensei Press. 123–150.

Nyberg, Henrik Samuel 1923. The Pahlavi documents from Avromān. *Le Monde Oriental* 17: 182–230.

Nyberg, Henrik Samuel 1974. *A Manual of Pahlavi* 2. *Glossary.* Wiesbaden: Otto Harrassowitz.

Okada, Hidehiro 1992. Mandarin, a language of the Manchus: How Altaic? In Gimm, Martin & Stary, Giovanni & Weiers, Michael eds. *Historische und bibliographische Studien zur Mandschuforschung.* Wiesbaden: Harrassowitz. 165–187.

Okell, John 1965. Nissaya Burmese. A case of adaptation to a foreign grammar and syntax. *Lingua* 15: 186–227.

Okell, John 1967. Nissaya Burmese. *Journal of the Burma Research Society* 50: 95–123.

Olach, Zsuzsanna 2013. *A Halich Karaim Translation of Hebrew Biblical Texts.* (Turcologica 98.) Wiesbaden: Harrassowitz.

Paccagnella, Ivano 1979. *Le macaronee padovane: Tradizione e lingua. Le macaronee padovane: Tradizione e lingua* [The Paduan Macaronee: Tradition and Language]. (Medioevo e umanesimo, 36.) Padova: Antenore.

Pakendorf, Brigitte 2007. *Contact in the Prehistory of the Sakha (Yakuts): Linguistic and Genetic Perspectives.* Leiden: Leiden University.

Pakendorf, Brigitte 2014. Paradigm copying in Tungusic: The Lamunkhin dialect of Èven and beyond. In Robbeets, Martine & Bisang, Walter eds. *Paradigm Change. In the Transeurasian Languages and Beyond.* (Studies in Language Companion Series 161). Amsterdam & Philadelphia: John Benjamins. 287–310.

Paoli, Ugo Enrico 1959. *Il latino maccheronico* [Macaronic Latin]. (Bibliotechina del Saggiatore 13.) Firenze: Felice Le Monnier.

Perini, Giorgio Bernardi 2001. Macaronica verba. Il divenire di una trasgressione linguistica ne seno dell'umanesimo [Macaronica verba. The emergence of a linguistic transgression in the bosom of humanism]. In Urso, Gianpaolo ed. *Integrazione/mescolanza/rifiuto: incontri di popoli, lingue e culture in Europa dall'antichità all'umanesimo.* (Centro recherche e documentazione sull'antichità classica: Monografie 22.) Roma. 327–336.

Poppe, Nicholaus N. 1973. Über einige Verbalstammbildungssuffixe in den altaischen Sprachen [On some suffixes deriving verbal stems in the Altaic languages]. *Orientalia Suecana* 21: 119–141.

Price, Glanville 2000. French in the Channel Islands. In Price Glanville ed. *Languages in Britain and Ireland.* Oxford: Basil Blackwell. 187–196.

Procházka, Stephan 2023. Turkish and Arabic. In Johanson, Lars ed. *Encyclopedia of Turkic Languages and Linguistics Online.* Brill.

Pruitt, William 1994. *Étude linguistique de nissaya birmans, traduction commentée de textes bouddhiques* [Linguistic Study of Burmese *nissaya*, Commented Translation of Buddhist Texts]. Paris: Presses de l'École francaise d'Extrème-Orient.

Rabinovitch, Judith N. 1996. An introduction to Hentai Kambun (variant Chinese), a hybrid Sinico-Japanese used by the male elite in premodern Japan. *Journal of Chinese Linguistics* 24: 98–127.

de Rachewiltz, Igor 1996. Hybrid Chinese of the Mongol period (13th–14th century). Wurm, Stephen & Mühlhäusler, Peter & Tryon, Darrell T. eds. *Atlas of Languages of Intercultural Communication in the Pacific, Asia, and the Americas* II.2. (Trends in Linguistics. Documentation 13.) Berlin & New York: De Gruyter. 905–906.

Rainey, Anson F. 1973. Reflections on the suffix conjugation in West-Semitized Amarna tablets. *Ugarit-Forchungen* 5: 235–262.

Rainey, Anson F. 1975. Morphology and the prefix tenses of West-Semitized 'Amarna Tablets'. *Ugarit-Forschungen* 7: 385–426.

Ramstedt, Gustaf J. 1912. Zur Verbalstammbildungslehre der mongolisch-türkischen Sprachen [On the theory of verbal stem formation in the Mongolic-Turkic languages]. *Journal de la Société Finno-Ougrienne* 28: 1–86.

Rehbein, Jochen & Herkenrath, Annette & Karakoç, Birsel 2009. Turkish in Germany: On contact-induced language change of an immigrant language in the multilingual landscape of Europe. *Language Typology and Universals* 62/3: 171–204.

Robbeets, Martine 2012. Shared verb morphology in the Transeurasian languages: Copy or cognate? In Johanson, Lars & Robbeets, Martine eds. *Copies Versus Cognates in Bound Morphology*. Brill: Leiden & Boston. 427–446.

Róna-Tas, András 1980. *On the earliest Samoyed-Turkish contacts*. Qongressus Quintus Internacionális Fenno-Ugristarun 1. Turku: Suomen Kielen Seura. 377–385.

Róna-Tas, András 1988. Turkic influence on the Uralic languages. In Sinor Denis ed. *Handbuch der Orientalistik* 8.1. *The Uralic Languages*. Leiden: Brill. 742–780.

Róna-Tas, András 1991. *An Introduction to Turkology*. Szeged: University of Szeged.

Ross, Malcolm 2001. Contact-induced change in Oceanic languages in north-west Melanesia. In Aikhenvald, Alexandra & Dixon R[obert]. M.W. eds. 2001. *Areal Diffusion and Genetic Inheritance: Problems in Comparative Linguistics*. Oxford: Oxford University Press. 134–166.

Ross, Malcolm 2005[2]. Metatypy. In Brown, Keith ed. *Encyclopedia of Languages and Linguistics*. Oxford: Elsevier. 95–99.

Sapir, Edward 1921. *Language. An Introduction to the Study of Speech*. New York: Harcourt, Brace and Company.

Schendl, Herbert 1996. Text types and code-switching in medieval and early modern English. *Vienna English Working Papers* 5: 50–62.

Schendl, Herbert 1997. 'To London fro Kent/Sunt predia depopulantes': Code-switching and medieval English macaronic poems. *Vienna English Working Papers* 6: 52–66.

Schmitt, Rüdiger 1991. *The Bisitun Inscriptions of Darius the Great. Old Persian Text.* (Corpus Inscriptionum Iranicarum 1.) London: School of Oriental and African Studies.

Shapira, Dan 2003. The Turkic languages and literatures. In Polliack, Meira ed. *Karaite Judaism. A Guide to its History and Literary Sources.* Leiden & Boston: Brill. 657–707.

Skjærvø, P. Oktor 1996. Aramaic Scripts for Iranian languages. In Daniels, Peter T. & Bright, William eds. *The World's Writing Systems.* Oxford & New York: Oxford University Press. 515–535.

Slobin, Dan I. 1980. The repeated path between transparency and opacity in language. In Studdert-Kennedy, Michael eds. *Signed and Spoken Language: Biological Constraint on Linguistic Form.* Weinheim: Verlag Chemie. 229–243.

von Soden, Wolfram & Wolfgang Röllig 1991[4]. *Das akkadische Syllabar* [The Akkadian Syllabary]. Rome: Biblical Institute Press.

Soper, John D. 1987. *Loan Syntax in Turkic and Iranian. The Verb Systems of Tajik, Uzbek, and Qashqay.* Ph.D. thesis. Los Angeles: University of California.

Stary, Giovanni 1985. Fundamental principles of Manchu poetry. In En-shean, Lin ed. *Proceedings of the International Conference on China Border Area Studies.* Taipei: National Chengchi University. 187–221.

Stolz, Thomas 2007. *Allora*: On the recurrence of funtion word borrowing in contact situatios with Italian. In Rehbein, Jochen et al. eds. *Connectivity in Grammar and Discourse.* Amsterdam & Philadelphia: Benjamins. 75–99.

Taylor, David G.K. 2002. Bilingualism and diglossia in late Antique Syria and Mesopotamia. In Adams, James N. & Janse, Mark & Swain, Simon eds. 2002. *Bilingualism in Ancient Society. Language Contact and the Written Text.* Oxford: Oxford University Press. 298–331.

Thomason, Sarah G. 1980. Morphological instability, with and without language contact. Fisiak, Jacek ed. *Historical Morphology.* The Hague: Mouton. 359–372.

Türker, Emel 2000. *Turkish–Norwegian Codeswitching. Evidence from Intermediate and Second Generation Turkish Immigrants in Norway.* (Acta Humaniora 83.) Oslo: University of Oslo.

Utas, Bo 1991. New Persian as an interethnic medium. In Svanberg, Ingvar ed. *Ethnicity, Minorities and Cultural Encounters.* (Uppsala Multiethnic Papers 25.) Uppsala: Uppsala University. 103–111.

Utas, Bo 2004. Semitic in Iranian: Written, read and spoken language. In Csató, Éva Á. & Isaksson, Bo & Jahani, Carina eds. *Linguistic Convergence and Areal Diffusion. Case Studies from Iranian, Semitic and Turkic.* London & New York: RoutledgeCurzon. 65–78.

Van Coetsem, Frans 2000. *A General and Unified Theory of the Transmission Process in Language Contact.* Heidelberg: Winter.

Wadley, Stephen A. 1991. *The Mixed-language Verses from the Manchu Dynasty in China.* (Papers on Inner Asia 16.) Bloomington: Indiana University Research Institute for Inner Asian Studies.

Wadley, Stephen A. 1996. Altaic influences on Beijing dialect: The Manchu case. *The Journal of the American Oriental Society* 116: 99–104.

Waley, Arthur 1957. Chinese-Mongol hybrid songs. *Bulletin of the School of Oriental and African Studies* 20: 581–584.

Weinreich, Uriel 1953. *Languages in Contact. Findings and Problems.* (Publications of the Linguistic Circle of New York 1.) New York: Linguistic Circle of New York.

Wenzel, Siegfried 1994. *Macaronic Sermons: Bililingualism and Preaching in Late-Medieval England.* (Recentiores: Later Latin Texts and Contexts.) Ann Arbor, Michigan: University of Michigan Press.

Windfuhr, Gernot L. 1979. *Persian Grammar. History and State of its Study.* Paris & New York: Mouton.

Windfuhr, Gernot L. 1982. The verbal category of inference in Persian. *Monumentum Georg Morgenstierne 2. Acta Iranica* 22: 263–287.

Wright, Laura C. 1995. A hypothesis on the structrure of macaronic business writing. In Fisiak, Jacek ed. *Medieval Dialectology.* (Trends in Linguistic Studies and Monographs 79.) Berlin: De Gruyter Mouton. 309–321.

Wright, Laura C. 1998. Mixed-language business writing: Five hundred years of codeswitching. In Jahr, Ernst Håkon ed. *Language Change: Advances in Historical Sociolinguistics.* (Trends in Linguistic Studies and Monographs 114.) Berlin: De Gruyter Mouton. 99–118.

Wright, Laura C. 2001a. Models of language mixing: Code-switching versus semicommunication in medieval Latin and Middle English accounts. In Kastovsky, Dieter & Arthur Mettinger eds. *Language Contact in the History of English.* Frankfurt am Main: Peter Lang. 363–376.

Wright, Laura C. 2001b. The role of international and national trade in the standardisation of English. In Moskowich-Spiegel, Fandino et al. eds. *Re-interpretations of English. Essays on Language, Linguistics and Philology* 1. A Coruna: Universidade da Coruna. 189–207.

Wright, Laura C. 2002a. Standard English and the lexicon: Why so many spellings? In Jones, Mari C. and Edith Esch eds. *Language Change: The Interplay of Internal, External and Extra-linguistic Factors.* Berlin: De Gruyter Mouton. 181–200.

Wright, Laura C. 2002b. Code-intermediate phenomena in medieval mixed-language business texts. *Language Sciences* 24: 471–489.

Wright, Laura C. 2005. Medieval mixed-language business texts and the rise of Standard English. In Skaffari, Janne et al. eds. *Opening Windows on Texts and Discourses of the Past.* (Pragmatics and Beyond, New Series 134.) Amsterdam: John Benjamins. 381–399.

Xelimskij, Evgenij A. 1996. 'Govorka'—the pidgin Russian of the Taymyr Peninsular area. In: Wurm, Stephen A. & Mühlhäusler, Peter & Tryon, Darrell T. (eds.) *Atlas of Languages of Intercultural Communication in the Pacific, Asia, and the Americas* 2: *Texts* (Trends in Linguistics. Documentation 13). Berlin & New York: De Gruyter Mouton. 1033–1034.

Yip, Moira Jean Winsland 2002. *Tone*. Cambridge: Cambridge University Press.

Zograf, Irina T. 1989. *Mongol'sko-kitajskaja interferencija. Jazyk mongol'skoj kanceljarii v Kitae* [Mongolic-Chinese Interference: The Language of the Mongol Chancellery in Cathay]. Moskva: Nauka.

Zunz, Leopold [Yom Tov Lipman Tsunts] 1832. *Die gottesdienstlichen Vorträge der Juden* [The Liturgical Speeches of the Jews]. Berlin: Asher.

Index of Subjects

Accommodation of copies   2–3, 6, 18, 35–36, 38–41, 59
Alloglottography   80, 82, 87, 116–118, 120–123
Attitudes   66–67, 70–71
Attractiveness   7–8, 12, 47, 56, 58, 73–74, 78

Code, types of
  Basic Code   1–8, 15, 19, 21–23, 29–30, 33, 37–39, 42–45, 49–50, 52, 68, 81–84, 88, 93, 106
  basic-code frame   3–4, 6–7, 18, 38, 49–50, 69, 83–84, 113
  foreign code   84, 86, 95, 106, 113, 125
  local code   9–12, 54, 58, 62, 81–82, 98–99
  Model Code   1–8, 21–23, 29–30, 37–39, 42–44, 51–52, 57, 72, 81–83
  primary code   1–2, 21, 57, 70, 84, 87, 89, 103–104
  recipient code   1, 38
  secondary code   1–2, 21, 87, 89
  strong vs. weak code   8, 14
Code-copying   1, 7, 9, 11, 37, 39, 52–53, 55, 60, 68–70, 72–73, 82, 85, 125
Code internal   6, 16, 23, 30, 36–37, 40, 43, 45, 49–50, 73, 76, 104
Code switching, code mixing   2–3, 69, 71, 85–86, 107
Cognate vs. copy   6, 72–78
Contact, family internal vs. family external   54–59, 104
Convergenc vs. divergence   1, 6, 13, 27, 50–51, 54, 56, 69
Copiability   7, 37, 39, 42–43, 54, 56, 73, 78
Copy, level of
  high copying   8–9, 50–51, 68–71, 80, 84, 93–94, 97
  low copying   70–71
Copy, types of
  bound morphemes   3, 5, 7, 18, 26, 31, 33–34, 38, 46–47, 72–74, 78, 92
  combinational   3–6, 18, 22–30, 32–36, 38–39, 45, 48–51, 62, 64, 72, 78, 96, 103
  conventionalized   49, 52–53, 83, 85
  frame-changing   7, 34, 68
  frequential   3–6, 22, 26, 29–32, 45, 59, 69, 72–74

  global   3–6, 18–20, 26, 28, 32–33, 35, 49, 51, 60, 62–64, 68–70, 74, 76
  habitualized   52–53
  material   3–6, 16, 21, 44, 49, 61, 72, 79, 96
  mixed   18, 28, 32–34
  momentary   52–53
  selective   3–6, 11, 16, 21–35, 38–39, 42, 48–53, 60–62, 68, 72, 74
  semantic   22, 45, 64, 72, 74, 79, 96, 103
Contact processes
  take-over copying   2, 9, 11–16, 19, 22, 54, 56, 58, 60, 68, 70, 81–84, 88–89, 91, 96, 100, 102
  carry-over copying   2, 5, 9–17, 19, 21, 47–48, 54, 56–58, 60, 62, 69, 81–82, 84–85, 98–100, 102–103, 113, 125
  shift   3, 9–10
Convergence vs. divergence   1, 6, 13, 27, 50–52, 54, 56, 69
Creativity of copying   6–7, 36

Frame   3–4, 6–7, 18, 34, 38, 49–50, 69, 83–84, 113

Globe, contact   5–6
Grammaticalization   19, 26, 30, 37–50, 79
  grammatical accommodation   39–41
  inherited grammaticalization   46–47
  source of grammaticalization   44
  target of grammaticalization   38, 44

Intertwining languages   8, 80, 82–83, 96, 106, 113, 124
Isomorphism   37–39, 41, 44, 46–48, 50, 68

Mixed language   14, 66, 70, 80, 83–84, 86, 88, 90–91, 94–95, 98, 100, 103, 105–113, 119, 125

Order of copying   5

Purism   40, 63, 66–67, 80, 82, 92, 95

Ranking, high vs. low/prestigous vs. less prestigous   80–125
Reading aid   86–87, 111–114

INDEX OF SUBJECTS

Remodeling   37, 42–43, 49–53

Stability   11, 56, 58, 65, 66–67, 73, 78–79, 111
Stratification
   superstrata   1, 9–10
   substrata   1, 9–13, 55–56, 58
   adstrata   1, 9–10, 13
Structuritis   8, 70

Target of copying   37–38, 42–44

Index of Languages and Language Families

Akkadian   84, 88–89, 118–120, 123–124
Altaic   27, 55, 72–79
Anatolian Turkish   82, 91
Arabic   5–7, 10, 26–27, 54–55, 60, 62–64, 81, 84, 87, 89–91, 93, 94–98, 106
Arabic-Persian   10, 26–27, 34, 54–55, 83, 91–98, 108
Aramaic   117, 119, 121–122
Arawak   40–41
Armenian   54, 106
Avestan   121–122
Azeri   11, 18–19, 21–28, 30–33, 54–55, 57, 91, 108, 117

Balkan Turkish   12, 28
Baniwa   40
Bashkir   13–16, 27
Basque   10, 45
Bulgarian   18, 48
Bulghar   13–15
Burmese   87, 112–114

Caucasian   12, 47, 54, 57
Celtic   9
Cèmuhi   42
Chaghatay   55, 63, 87, 90, 96–98
Chinese   51, 54, 60–62, 85–87, 99–104, 109, 111–113, 117, 123–124
Chuvash   11, 13–17, 47, 55, 57–58, 75
Crimean Romani   13
Crimean Tatar   13, 68

Danish   25
Drubéa   42
Dutch   10, 26, 29, 35

East Middle Turkic   97
East Old Turkic   28, 54, 56, 75, 77
Eblaite   118
Elamite   85, 87, 119–120
English   1–2, 4–5, 10, 26, 29, 35–36, 51–52, 60–63, 66, 70, 81, 83, 94, 99, 109–111, 125
Evenki   11, 55, 58

Finno-Permic   13–14
Finno-Ugric   13, 15, 17, 57
French   9–10, 42, 46, 60, 83, 105, 107, 109, 111

Gagauz   5, 28, 55, 68, 70
Gaulish   9–10
Georgian   117
German   1–3, 22–23, 25–26, 34–36, 51, 81, 84, 95, 105, 107
Germanic   9–10, 45, 111
Germany Turkish   3, 5, 22–23, 34–36, 70
Govorka   64
Greek   12, 21, 54–55, 72, 85–87, 105–106, 122

Hattic   119
Hebrew   62, 84, 86–88, 96, 109, 114–116
Hittite   119
Hungarian   3–4, 21, 51
Hurrian   119

Indic   98–99, 112, 114
Indo-European   10–11, 13, 54, 56, 61, 89–90, 112, 119–120
Iranian   18, 27–28, 54, 56–57, 89–91, 121–122
Irano-Turkic   18–25, 28, 30–34, 54
Irish   10

Japanese   74–75, 77, 79, 85, 87, 100–102, 111–113, 117, 123–124

Kalmyk   13
Kanaanite   88
Karachay-Balkar   12
Karaim   2, 4, 12, 21, 43–44, 55, 59, 67–71, 78, 87, 114–116
Karakhanid   54, 56, 97
Kashkay   18, 21, 25
Kazakh   26, 55, 58
Kazan Tatar   14
Khakas   27
Khalaj   18–19, 21, 24, 26, 31–33
Khorasan Turkic   19, 21, 31, 108
Khotanese   89
Khwarezmian   89
Kipchak   13–17, 47–48, 68, 97, 114
Kirghiz   26, 55
Komi   13
Korean   74–75, 79, 112
Kurdish   30

INDEX OF LANGUAGES AND LANGUAGE FAMILIES

Latin   46, 63–64, 81–82, 84, 87, 99, 105, 107, 109–111, 117
Lithuanian   69, 116
Luvian   119

Macedonian   23
Maku   40
Malay   62
Manchu   85–86, 103–104, 109
Mandarin   61–62
Mari   11, 13–15, 17, 57
Middle Chinese   61
Middle Iranian   87, 89, 121
Mishar Tatar   14
Mongolian   85, 98, 102–103
Mongolic   13, 54–58, 74–75
Mordva   13–15

Nenets   13
New Persian   84, 89–96
Noghay   54
Norn   9
Norwegian   4, 21, 25, 35

Ob-Ugric   14
Oghur   54, 57
Oghuz Turkic   21, 57, 70, 91, 97, 98
Old English   60
Old Norse   60
Old Persian   85, 87, 120–122
Old Uyghur   55
Ottoman Turkish   8, 18, 31, 55, 63, 83–84, 87, 90–96, 114

Pali   87, 112–114
Parthian   119, 122
Persian   11, 18–22, 24–28, 30–34, 48, 54–57, 82, 84, 90–98, 106–108, 113, 121–122
Phoenician   88
Polish   69, 116
Portuguese   10, 41, 46, 50
Prākrit   85, 98–99, 112
Proto Turkic   55
Proto-Germanic   10

Romance   10, 45–46, 60, 63, 83, 86, 94, 109, 111
Romani   12–13
Russian   2, 13, 15, 26–27, 34, 44, 55, 59–60, 64–65, 69, 71, 97, 116

Samoyedic   13, 54, 64
Sanskrit   85, 98–99, 112, 114
Sayan Turkic   55
Scots dialect   9
Semitic   62, 84, 87–90, 93, 117–122
Siberian Turkic   26–27, 58
Sinhalese   87, 114
Slavic   4, 12, 18, 21, 26–27, 43, 47–48, 54–55, 59, 69, 96, 116
Soghdian   54, 56, 89
South Oghuz   21
South-Siberian Turkic   12
Spanish   10, 46, 51, 63–64, 106
Sumerian   117–120, 123
Syriac   86–87
Swedish   2, 4, 21, 25, 35–36, 51–52, 61, 65

Tajik   2
Tamil   62
Tariana   40–41, 50, 27, 55
Tatar   13, 15–16
Tayo   42
Tokharian   56, 89
Transeurasian   46–47, 55
Tucano   40–41
Tungusic   11–12, 54–58, 64, 74–75, 103
Turkic   2, 4–5, 7, 10–27, 30–34, 38, 43, 47, 54–59, 63–64, 67–70, 74–75, 78–79, 83–84, 89, 91–98, 106–108, 113–116
Turkish   3, 5–6, 12–13, 18, 21–27, 30, 33–36, 55, 58, 70, 83, 91–96, 108
Turkmen   27, 55, 91

Udmurt   13–15
Ugaritic   120
Uralic   10, 54
Urdu   90, 108
Urum   55
Uyghur   11–12, 27, 55–56, 58, 62, 97–98
Uzbek   11, 19, 55–57, 97

Volga Bulghar   13, 17

West Rumelian Turkish   21, 23

Yakut   11, 47, 55, 57–58
Yiddish   84, 96

Index of Personal Names

Adamou, Evangelia 13
Adams, James 85
Adelaar, Willem F.H. 39
Aikhenvald, Alexandra 37–39, 41, 50, 70
Austin, Peter 67

Backus, Ad 23
Baki, Ablimit 62
Bakker, Peter 80
Baskakov, Nikolaj A. 27
Baumgarten, Jean 84
Bechert, Heinz 114
Benzing, Johannes 79
Berberian, Haig 106
Berta, Árpád 16
Birnbaum, Solomon 84
Böhl, Franz Marius Theodor 88
Bodrogligeti, András J. 97
Bohnacker, Ute 35
Browne, Edward Granville 106
Brendemoen, Bernt 29
Bulut, Christiane 26, 91

Caferoğlu, Ahmed 108
Civil, Michael 118, 123
Clyne, Michael 29, 50
Colonna, Francesco 105
Comrie, Bernard 27, 50, 56, 74
Corne, Chris 37, 42
Coulmas, Florian 123
Csató, Éva Á. 1, 28, 37, 44, 55, 67, 69–70, 91, 116

Dankoff, Robert 93
Dixon, Robert M.W. 37–38, 83
Doerfer, Gerhard 75–76
Dolatkhah, Sohrab 18, 25

Eckman, János 97
Edgerton, Franklin 98
Elwert, Wilhelm Theodor 106
Erdal, Marcel 75, 77

Fewster, Penelope 85
Forster, Leonard 106–107
Fragner, Bert G. 90

Gabain, Annemarie von 28
Gardani, Francesco 7
Gershevitch, Ilya 116, 120–121
Gianto, Agustinus 88
Gorelova, Liliya M. 104
Griffiths, Paul J. 99
Grünewald, August 107

Haenisch, Erich 104
Heine, Bernd 29–30, 37–38, 42, 45
Helander, Hans 81
Henning, Walter B. 121
Henrici, Emil 107
Herkenrath, Annette 5, 22
von Hinüber, Oskar 112

Igla, Birgit 12
Ikeda, Jun 123
Izre'el, Shlomo 88

Jacobs, Neil G. 84, 96
Jespersen, Otto 83–84, 94
Johanson, Lars 1, 8, 11, 18, 20, 22–23, 25–27, 29–30, 32–34, 37–38, 47–48, 50–51, 56–57, 67, 70, 72–79, 82, 90–91, 93, 108
Joseph, Brian 73

Karakoç, Birsel 5, 22, 24, 35
Katz, Dovid 84
Kıral, Filiz 18
Kloss, Heinz 108
Knudtzon, Jørgen Alexander 88
Köprülü, M. Fuad 108
Kossmann, Maarten G. 88
Kowalski, Tadeusz 12, 58, 116
Kuteva, Tania 37–38, 42, 45

Langslow, David R. 120
Lazar, Moshé 109
Lewis, Geoffrey 92
Li, Charles 104
Lutz, Angelika 60

Malmqvist, Göran 61
Mansuroğlu, Mecdud 91
Matras, Yaron 1, 7, 13, 39, 80

INDEX OF PERSONAL NAMES

Meisig, Konrad   90, 114
Menges, Karl H.   75
Menz, Astrid   28, 70
Miller, Roy Andrew   74–75, 77, 79, 100–101
Minegishi, Akira   100
Moran, William L.   88
Mosel, Ulrike   66
Mous, Marten   80
Müller, Otto   107
Musaev, Kenesbaj M.   116
Muyskin, Peter   3

Németh, Julius   95
Nevins, Andrew   69
Numamoto, Katsuaki   111
Nyberg, Henrik Samuel   122

Okada, Hidehiro   104
Okell, John   112–113
Olach, Zsuzsanna   115

Paccagnella, Ivano   105
Pakendorf, Birgitte   11–12
Paoli, Ugo Enrico   105
Perini, Giorgio Bernardi   105
Poppe, Nicholaus N.   74–75
Price, Glanville   109
Procházka, Stephan   8
Pruitt, William   112

Rabinovitch, Judith N.   100–102
de Rachewiltz, Igor   102–103
Rainey, Anson F.   88
Ramstedt, Gustaf J.   74–77
Rehbein, Jochen   22
Robbeets, Martine   1, 46, 72–73, 100
Róna-Tas, András   54

Ross, Malcolm   1

Sapir, Edward   37, 46
Schendl, Herbert   109
Schmitt, Rüdiger   120
Shapira, Dan   115
Skjærvø, P. Oktor   121
Slobin, Dan   7
von Soden, Wolfram   119
Soper, John D.   18
Stary, Giovanni   109
Stolz, Thomas   7

Taylor, David G.K.   87
Thomason, Sarah G.   78–79
Thompson, Sandra A.   104
Türker, Emel   25

Utas, Bo   90, 122

Van Coetsem, Frans   1
Vaux, Bert   69

Wadley, Stephen A.   104
Waley, Arhur   103
Weinreich, Uriel   52
Wenzel, Siegfried   105
Windfuhr, Gernot L.   31, 48
Wright, Laura C.   110

Xelimskij, Evgenij A.   64–65

Yip, Moira Jean Winsland   62

Zograf, Irina T.   102
Zunz, Leopold   84